CRANKARM AND CHAINRINGS

D0200098

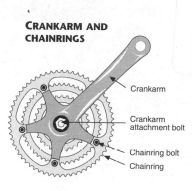

Crankarm

Crankarm
attachment bolt

Chainring bolt

Chainring

THUMB SHIFTER

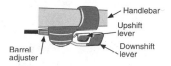

Barrel
adjuster

Shift lever

Handlebar

STANDARD PEDAL

Pedal body

Pedal axle

Pedal cage

UNDER-THE-BAR SHIFTER

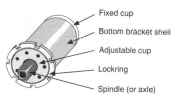

Handlebar

Upshift
lever

Downshift
lever

Barrel
adjuster

CLIPLESS PEDAL

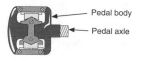

Pedal body

Pedal axle

BOTTOM BRACKET

Fixed cup

Bottom bracket shell

Adjustable cup

Lockring

Spindle (or axle)

MOUNTAIN BIKE EMERGENCY REPAIR

Tim Toyoshima

THE
MOUNTAINEERS

Published by
The Mountaineers
1001 SW Klickitat Way
Seattle, Washington 98134

9 8 7 6
5 4 3 2

Published simultaneously in Canada by Douglas & McIntyre, Ltd., 1615 Venables Street, Vancouver, B.C. V5L 2H1

Published simultaneously in Great Britain by Cordee, 3a DeMontfort Street, Leicester, England, LE1 7HD

Manufactured in the United States of America

Edited by Christine Clifton-Thornton

Illustrations by Coleman Design

Cover design by Dorothy Wachtenheim Design

Book design and typesetting by The Mountaineers Books

Cover photograph: Mountain bike repair at Slickrock, Utah
© Karl Weatherly/Allstock

Library of Congress Cataloging-in-Publication Data
Toyoshima, Tim.
    Mountain bike emergency repair / Tim Toyoshima.
       p.   cm.
    Includes index.
    ISBN 0-89886-422-4
    All terrain bicycles—Maintenance and repair—
Handbooks, manuals, etc. I. Title.
TL430.T69 1995
629.28'772--dc20
                                  94-44409
                                    CIP

CONTENTS

Before You Hit the Trail 9

Looking for Trouble .. 11

Top Ten Maintenance
Tips 12

**Inspecting Your Bike
After a Crash** 15

Seven-Point Post-Crash
Inspection 16

Tools and Parts 18

Seven Survival Tools ... 19

Expedition Parts and
Tools 22

Tools for Different Trail
Conditions 27

Carrying It All 28

Troubleshooting 29

Bottom Bracket 29

Loose Bottom Bracket .. 29

Tight or Seized Bottom
Bracket 30

**Brakes and Brake
Levers** 30

Brake Pads Rub Against
Rim 30

Brake Pads Rub Against
Tire or Slide Off
Rim 31

Brakes Stick 31

Brakes Squeal 32

Little or No Braking
Power 33

Broken Cantilever
Spring 34

Broken Brake Lever 34

**Crankarms and
Pedals** 34

Loose Crankarm 34

Crankarm Has Fallen
Off 35

Rounded Crankarm
Hole 36

Bent Crankarm 37

Lost Chainring Bolts ... 38

Loose Chainring 38

Bent Big Chainring 38

Bent Small Chainring .. 39

Broken Pedal Cage 40

Can't Release Shoe
From a Shimano
SPD Pedal 41

5

6 ◆ Contents

Frame and Fork 41
Bent Fork 41
Bent or Broken Frame .. 42
Headsets 43
Loose Headset 43
Tight Headset 43
Cracked Headset 44
**Shifters, Derailleurs,
and Chains** 44
Index Shifting Skips or
Doesn't Shift (Rear
Derailleur) 44
Index Shifting Doesn't
Shift or Chain Rubs
(Front Derailleur) ... 46
Bent Rear Derailleur Cage
or Derailleur
Hanger 48
Broken Rear
Derailleur 49
Broken Rear Derailleur
Pulley Wheels 50
Broken Derailleur
Cable 50
Chain Falls Off Big
Chainring 51
Chain Falls Off Small
Chainring 52
Chain Falls Off Small
Cog 53
Chain Falls Off Large
Cog 53

Broken Chain 54
Squeaky Chain 56
Chain Skips 56
Chain Has a Tight
Link 57
Jammed Chain 58
Tires and Tubes 58
Flat Tire 58
Ripped Sidewall 59
No Tubes or Patches ... 60
Broken Bead on Tire ... 61
No Tire Levers 62
Tire Bead Blows Out
From Rim 62
Pump Doesn't Work ... 63
Wheels and Hubs 64
Dented Rim 64
Bent Rim: Bends, Tacos,
and Potato Chips ... 65
Broken Freewheel 67
Locked Freewheel 67
Bent or Broken Axle 68
Loose Hub 68
Loose Spoke 69
Broken Spoke 69
Broken Quick Release .. 70
Miscellaneous 71
Broken Handlebar 71
Handlebar and Stem
Turned in the Steerer
Tube 72
Broken Seat Post 72

Broken Seat 73
Broken Seat Binder
    Bolt 73
Broken Stem 74

Real Repairs 75

Bottom Bracket 75
Adjusting a Bottom
    Bracket 75
Brakes 76
Centering Cantilever
    Brakes, U-Brakes, and
    Power Cams 76
Adjusting Brake Pads .. 78
Adjusting Brake Cable
    Tension 80
Replacing a Brake
    Cable 81
Chains 82
Freeing a Jammed
    Chain 82
Installing a Chain 83
Derailleurs 85
Adjusting a Front
    Derailleur 85
Adjusting Index Shifting
    (Front Derailleur) ... 87
Adjusting a Rear
    Derailleur 88
Adusting Index Shifting
    (Rear Derailleur) 90

Replacing a Broken Pulley
    Wheel on the Rear
    Derailleur 91
Replacing a Rear
    Derailleur 92
Replacing a Derailleur
    Cable 92
Headsets 93
Adjusting a Headset 93
Hubs 94
Adjusting a Hub 94
Replacing an Axle 95
Tubes and Tires 96
Finding the Cause of a
    Flat Tire 96
Finding Punctures in a
    Tube 98
Fixing a Flat Tire 98
Patching a Tube 99
**Wheels, Spokes, and
Freewheels** 101
Removing and Installing
    a Wheel 101
Truing a Wheel 101
Replacing a Spoke 104
Removing and Replacing
    a Freewheel 106

Index 108

BEFORE YOU HIT THE TRAIL . . .

Fixing your mountain bike is simple—if you see someone else do a repair a couple of times, you usually can get the hang of it. The trouble is that most people run into mechanical problems before they see their particular problem repaired. Bad things just don't happen very often, and most people think about repairs only when something is broken. Unfortunately, the key to fixing your mountain bike quickly and effectively—especially when you are out on the trail—is experience. You've got to know how to find the cause of a problem, choose the appropriate repair, and then do the repair. For on-trail repairs, you also need to know what tools and parts to bring with you in order to make repairs, and you need to know what to do if you don't have those tools.

You can get experience by working as a bike mechanic, by finding out the hard way by riding and fixing your bike a lot, or by getting a good book—like this one. This book is virtual experience—all the good tips without the pain and frustration of trying to find the most efficient way to fix things on your own. If something goes wrong with your bike in the

9

middle of nowhere, this book will certainly help you, especially if you bring the right tools.

This book is structured to help you fix your bike fast.

This chapter gives you some quick tips on how you can prevent most problems from happening through simple maintenance, tells you how to look for damage after a crash, and lists the tools that you should take with you.

The next chapter, Troubleshooting, contains descriptions of problems (and their symptoms) and instructions for fixing those problems. The instructions provide two types of repairs.

Emergency repairs. For these repairs, it is assumed that you have the seven survival tools (see the Tools and Parts section) or no tools at all. An emergency repair often lists a number of alternatives to fixing a problem, starting with repairs that use one or more of the seven survival tools and ending with repairs that require either no tools at all or items that you can find on your bike, your clothing, or the trail. Usually an emergency repair will fix your bike to the point that you can ride back to the trailhead (instead of having to walk back, dragging broken bike parts), although often the repair will be stable enough so that you can finish out your ride.

Permanent repairs. These may require tools or spare parts beyond the seven survival tools. A permanent repair will fix the problem to the extent that you will be able to finish out your ride, but sometimes a more intensive repair will have to be made after your ride in order for optimum bike performance. This instruction also tells you what to replace or fix when you get home so that the problem will be fixed for good.

The final chapter, Real Repairs, provides instructions for making the most common repairs, and also gives you tips on how to check the adjustment of parts on your bike. If you know exactly *what* you need to fix, but you don't know *how*, you may want to look at the final chapter first.

The problems and repairs are grouped together by component or general mechanical area such as chain, derailleurs, brakes, wheels, and so on.

Use the diagrams at the beginning and end of the book if you can't find the right word to describe a part on your bike. These diagrams show and label the key parts of the components and serve as a visual glossary.

One thing that this book doesn't cover is suspension. There are many manufacturers and models available, and each one has its own nuances. If you want to experiment with or fine-tune your suspension, you should do this at home, before you go to the trail. If your suspension is tuned before you hit the trail, you will probably never have any problems with it during a ride.

Your best bet is to follow the instructions for your suspension system, which usually give some general recommendations for tuning according to your weight and the type of riding you do. If you have an air/oil-type fork, make sure that the air pressure is at the recommended pressure. If you are going on a long trip, you may want to take any special adjustment wrenches or air pumps (and the manual) with you.

This book has solutions to many problems. but there are some things you just can't fix out on the trail: broken fork; broken frame; broken crankarm; broken bottom bracket axle; broken stem body; cracked rim; broken pedal axle.

Looking for Trouble

You often can avoid problems before you begin your ride. By inspecting your bike and performing some simple pre-ride maintenance, you'll have fewer repairs to perform on the trail.

Top Ten Maintenance Tips

Things generally don't just break or go out of adjustment in the middle of a ride. There usually are signs of wear or poor adjustment that you can detect on close examination. You can avoid most of the pain-in-the-butt, desperation repairs in this book by checking your bike and doing simple maintenance and fixes at home before you hit the trail.

1. Tires. Check tire pressure. Low tire pressure is a great way to get a pinch flat or a dented rim. Make sure that you have the appropriate air pressure for the terrain on your ride and for your weight. While you're at it, check the tires for cuts.

2. Cables. Check brake and derailleur cables for frayed strands. If one strand of a cable has broken at a friction point (such as the cable guide beneath your bottom bracket), you can bet that more strands will break as you use the cable. Also, if you feel binding or excessive resistance in a cable when you shift or brake, the cable may be frayed within the cable housing or it may be dry or even rusted and in need of lubrication.

If a cable is frayed, replace it (see Replacing a Brake Cable—or Replacing a Derailleur Cable—in the Real Repairs chapter).

3. Spoke tension. Check the spoke tension on both wheels. All spokes on a wheel should have approximately the same tension. If a spoke is so loose that it rattles, or it is overly tight, the rim may be dented, bent, or cracked. While you're checking the spokes, spin the wheels and make sure that the rim spins smoothly between the brake pads. If the rim rubs, check for rim damage (see the sections Dented Rim and Bent Rim: Bends, Tacos, and Potato Chips, in the Troubleshooting chapter). True the rim if the rim isn't damaged (see Truing a Wheel, in the Real Repairs chapter).

4. Headset adjustment. Check the headset for play (looseness) or binding (tightness). A loose headset can damage both the headset and the steerer tube of the fork. Worse yet, it may cause poor handling and braking. Check the lock-nut. If you can turn it with your hand, the headset is loose or on its way to becoming loose.

To check for a loose headset, hold the front brake so that the front wheel can't turn and move the bike back and forth. The headset is loose if you can see the headset rock forward and back (way too loose) or if you can feel the headset knock as you rock the bike.

To check for a tight or bernelled headset, lift the bike off the ground. Turn the handlebar from side to side. If you feel binding or roughness (feels like small bumps as you turn the handlebar), the headset probably is too tight; adjust the headset (see Adjusting a Headset, in the Real Repairs chapter). If the handlebar slightly locks into position when the bar is straight (feels like it clicks into a notch), you have bernelling (indentations in the headset cups created by the pressure or wear of the bearings) on your headset. To confirm this, turn the handlebar side to side—you will feel the headset click on the notch. Replace the headset.

5. Bottom bracket adjustment. Check the bottom bracket for play. A loose bottom bracket can damage or cause excessive wear on both the bottom bracket spindle and the bearing cups. A loose bottom bracket also can cause shifting problems.

To check for a loose bottom bracket, grasp both crankarms and try moving them laterally. If you feel knocking as you move them from side to side, the bottom bracket probably is loose or one of the crankarms may be loose. Adjust the bottom bracket (see Adjusting a Bottom Bracket, in the Real Repairs chapter).

6. Brake pad wear. Check the brake pads for wear and

proper alignment. Make sure that the brake pads have not worn past the wear indicators on the brake pads. Most brake pads have a mark on the pad that indicates that the pad needs to be replaced; others have vertical grooves in the brake pad surface and these pads are worn out when they have worn past the grooves. If your pads are worn, replace and adjust them (see Adjusting Brake Pads, in the Real Repairs chapter).

Make sure that the brake pads contact the rim properly. They should not rub on the tire (this will cause tire wear and eventually tear the sidewall of the tire), and they should not ride above the rim (brake pads may slip off the rim when braking hard). The brake pads also should make flush contact with the rim.

7. Chain. Lubricate the chain. A dry chain causes extra wear on the chain, freewheel, and chainrings. An over-lubed chain attracts dirt, also causing extra wear. Make sure that your chain is lubed but not smothered; wipe off extra lubricant with a rag. For details on properly lubing a chain, see Squeaky Chain, in the Troubleshooting chapter.

8. Hub adjustment. Check the hubs for play or binding. A loose or tight hub can cause excessive wear on the bearings, cups, and cones of the hub. A loose hub can cause a bent or broken axle. A loose hub also can affect the handling of the bike.

To check for a loose hub on a wheel, try to move the rim laterally between the two brake pads. If the hub has play (you can feel the rim move from side to side), the hub is loose and its cones need to be tightened. Adjust the hub (see Adjusting a Hub, in the Real Repairs chapter). A loose hub also may be the sign of a broken axle. If the axle is broken, replace it (see Replacing an Axle, in the Real Repairs chapter).

To check for a tight hub, lift the wheel off the ground and

gently spin it. If the wheel stops abruptly, or if you can feel binding as the wheel spins, the hub may be too tight. Adjust the hub (see Adjusting a Hub, in the Real Repairs chapter).

9. Crankarms. Check that the crankarms are tight. A loose crankarm can ruin your crankarm by rounding out the bevelled hole that connects it to the bottom bracket axle. If this happens, the crankarm may eventually fall off your bike. To check for a loose crankarm, grasp one crankarm and try to move it laterally. If the crankarm moves on the bottom bracket axle (you can see it move or feel it knock), the crankarm is loose and needs to be tightened. You may want to remove it and check to see if the crankarm hole has been rounded (a normal crankarm hole is square or octagonal). If it has been rounded, replace the crankarm or shim the hole (add extra material to create a snugger fit); see Loose Crankarm, in the Troubleshooting chapter.

10. Seat bolt. Check that the seat bolt (the bolt that holds the seat to the seat post) is tight.

Inspecting Your Bike After a Crash

Mountain biking usually takes place on rough and sometimes unpredictable terrain. Your chances of crashing are much higher than if you ride a road bike on a smooth, paved highway. Crashes can damage your bike or force it out of adjustment. After a crash, always inspect your bike for damage (after you check to make sure that you're in one piece yourself). The damage can sometimes be enough to make the bike unsafe to ride.

Crashing is bad enough the first time. Avoid another crash—use this seven-point inspection to prevent further damage to your bike and yourself.

Seven-Point Post-Crash Inspection

1. Frame. Check for bent or cracked tubes. Chipping, blistering, bubbling, or wrinkling in the paint often indicate bends or cracks in the frame tubes. Run your finger carefully over these areas to check for bends or cracks beneath the paint. Small dents usually are rideable. Cracks are dangerous because they usually get larger from the stress of riding. If you choose to ride with a cracked frame, check the crack periodically to be sure it is not getting bigger.

A severe bend, break, or crack can affect the handling and structural integrity of the bike. If your bike has one of these severe defects, you probably should walk the bike, but if you choose to ride, do so very slowly and carefully, and dismount for steep descents.

Regardless of the size of a dent, bend, or crack, have your frame checked and repaired at a bike shop that also offers a frameshop, or by a custom framebuilder.

2. Fork. Check that there are no bends or cracks in the fork and that the fork blades are not bent back. Make sure that you can turn the handlebar left and right without the front wheel hitting the downtube. When you turn the bar left and right, make sure that there is no binding in the headset. Binding in the headset can mean a bent steerer tube or headtube. If there are any bends or cracks in the fork, it must be replaced. Avoid riding with a damaged fork: think of riding along and then having someone suddenly take your front wheel away—you guessed it, face plant, or worse, brain damage.

3. Wheels. Check each wheel. To check for bends, use one brake pad as a reference point, spin the wheel slowly, and see if the rim moves back and forth in relation to the brake pad. If the rim wobbles back and forth or periodically contacts the rim, you need to true the wheel (see Truing a Wheel, in the Real Repairs chapter) or perform one of the drastic fixes for a bent rim (see Bent Rim: Bends, Tacos, and Potato Chips, in the Troubleshooting chapter). To check for flat spots, look at the wheel in profile. Using one brake pad as a reference point, spin the wheel, and see if the rim moves up and down in relation to the brake pad. If the rim moves up and down, the wheel is not perfectly round and may have a flat spot (see the section Dented Rim, in the Troubleshooting chapter).

Check that the wheels are mounted properly in the dropouts.

Check that the quick release levers for each wheel are closed.

4. Handlebar. Check for cracks or dents in the bar. If you find a large crack or dent, treat the bar as a broken handlebar and try reinforcing it (see Broken Handlebar, in the Troubleshooting chapter). Check for bends in the bar. Make sure that the stem has not turned in the steerer tube. Stand over the bike to see that the bar forms a 90-degree angle with your front tire. If it doesn't, your steering will be affected (see Handlebar and Stem Turned in the Steerer Tube, in the Troubleshooting chapter).

5. Crankarms. Check the crankarms to make sure that they are not bent. If you test-ride the bike, you may feel unusual rotation in the pedal (feels like the pedal is squirming beneath your foot). This may be caused by a bent pedal axle or a bent crankarm (see Bent Crankarm, in the Troubleshooting chapter). Also check to make sure that the chainrings are not bent and that no chainring teeth are bent. To check for a bent chainring or bent teeth, turn the crankarms and watch the chainring. If the chainring or any of its teeth wobble back and forth laterally, the chainring or teeth are bent (see the sections Bent Big Chainring and Bent Small

Chainring, in the Troubleshooting chapter).

6. Rear derailleur. Check that the rear derailleur cage is straight (not bent out or bent in). If the cage looks like it is bent in, check the rear derailleur hanger. To see if the derailleur cage is bent into the spokes, lift the rear wheel, turn the pedals with one hand, and shift gears with the rear derailleur one gear at a time up to the large cog. If you hear or see the derailleur cage hitting the spokes, stop. The rear derailleur cage or hanger is bent (see Bent Rear Derailleur Cage or Derailleur Hanger, in the Troubleshooting chapter).

7. Brakes. Make sure that the cables, cable housing, and straddle cables are connected and seated correctly. A crash can knock straddle cables loose from the straddle hanger or the quick release, and cable housings can be knocked out of their cable stops. Make sure that the brake levers work (not bent or cracked).

Tools and Parts

Although all repairs outlined in this book can be done on the trail, some of the more detailed repairs in the Real Repairs chapter cannot be done without some of the following tools. Therefore, the usefulness of some of the more detailed repairs is in direct proportion to whether or not you've packed all the right tools.

How many tools and how much extra equipment you take depends on how long and how far you plan to ride. The longer you are out on the trail the greater the chance that something will go wrong; and the farther you are from civilization, the less you want to walk back. So the longer your trip, the more tools and spare parts you will want to take with you.

Because a mountain bike rider often encounters natural

obstacles (logs, rocks, etc.) and rough terrain, the bike takes a lot of abuse—parts can work loose, parts can wear out over the course of long trip, and parts can be damaged in a crash.

With the Seven Survival Tools, you should be able to handle the most common on-trail repairs and perform make-shift fixes to most other problems. You should carry these seven tools whenever you go for a ride.

Seven Survival Tools

1. Spare tube(s) and patch kit. A patch kit enables you to fix small to moderate punctures in a tube. You can patch most punctures. But occasionally, you'll have cuts too big to patch, more holes than patches, or a broken valve. In these cases, you'll need a new tube. It's also a lot easier and faster to replace a tube than to patch a puncture. However, you can run out of tubes fast on a rocky or thorny trail (or on a really unlucky day).

To be safe, you should bring both a spare tube (two or more on a long trip) and a patch kit. Use the tubes first and then use the patch kit when you start getting desperate. Make sure that you carry a spare that has the type of valve that works with your pump. It's a good idea to have the same type of valve on your spares as you do on the tubes already installed on your bike.

2. Tire levers. Tire levers are used to take a tire off the rim so that you can fix a puncture or replace the tire. Some tires have a loose enough fit so that you can take them off using only your hands; some tires (a few foldable models come to mind) are torture or nearly impossible to get off without tire levers.

3. Pump. You need a pump to inflate tires after you fix a flat and to add more pressure to your tires if necessary. Make sure that your pump takes the type of valve you have on your bike (and on your spare tubes). There are two types of valves. Schraeder valves are the type you find on car tires and most mountain bikes. Presta valves are the type you find on road racing bikes and on high-end mountain bikes. Some pumps have a fitting that you can reverse so you can pump both valve types.

4. Chain tool. Using a chain tool, you can break a chain (to remove a chain jammed between the chainrings and frame, for example), remove damaged links, and rejoin a broken chain. You can also use a chain tool to make your bike rideable after destroying your rear derailleur.

If you have a Shimano Hyperglide chain, be aware that you will need a special chain tool and special pins to break or rejoin the chain.

5. Allen wrench set. If you have a set of 3-, 4-, 5-, and 6-millimeter allen wrenches, you'll be able tighten and adjust most (if not all) allen bolts on your bike.

Common Allen Wrench Sizes and Uses

Size (mm)	Common Uses
2	Brake-pad centering for Shimano cantilevers and U-Brakes
3	Release tension of SPD pedals
4	Water bottle cage bolts and some brake and derailleur cable attachment bolts
5	Chainring bolts, front derailleur mounting clamp, cantilever brake mounting bolt, seat binder bolts, handlebar clamp bolts, some straddle cable hangers, and some brake and derailleur cable attachment bolts
6	Handlebar stem bolt and rear derailleur mounting bolt

7	Campagnolo crankarm bolts
8	Shimano crankarm bolts
10	Shimano freehub bolts

6. Adjustable wrench. A 6-inch adjustable wrench can loosen and tighten nuts and bolts; straighten bent chainrings, bent rear derailleur hangers, bent front derailleur cages, and bent pedal cages; and be used in an emergency as a spoke wrench.

Don't bother getting an adjustable wrench larger than 6 inches. A 14-inch adjustable wrench can be used as a headset wrench, hammer, a great lever for turning a freewheel tool, and a superior weapon in case of alien or animal attack—but it's big and heavy. If you want to haul it, go ahead.

7. Duct tape. If it's broken, ripped, or cracked, you often can use duct tape to temporarily fix or reattach whatever it is. Duct tape can be used as a boot for a torn sidewall or a reinforcement for splinting a broken frame, seat post, or handlebar. It also can be used to reattach a broken seat or rack.

To cut down on weight, carry duct tape wrapped around your ziplocked tool sheath (see Carrying It All, near the end of this chapter), or wrap it around a film canister and use the film canister to carry your aspirin, allergy medicine, spare nuts and bolts, matches, etc.

7½. Survival stuff. If you get lost, the essentials for survival (food, water, warmth, and protection from the elements) may be the difference between life and death. Bring extra food and water, an emergency blanket (one of the Mylar, folding kind), a flashlight, and matches. The key to survival, of course, is in knowing your route and starting your ride early enough in the day to finish before dark.

Expedition Parts and Tools

When you use your mountain bike for long day trips or for camping, you *really* want to avoid having to walk your bike back to civilization. The following tools and parts (along with the Seven Survival Tools) will enable you to fix just about anything and keep on riding.

Screwdrivers. A Phillips head screwdriver can be used to adjust both the front and rear derailleurs. A standard flat head screwdriver can be used as a chisel, used as a mini crowbar, or even used to tighten screws. You'll find that a flat head screwdriver can be used to repair your bike in ways you never imagined.

Crankarm wrench. A crankarm wrench tightens the crankarms to the bottom bracket spindle. On rough terrain, or if you tax the crankarms through heavy use, the crankarms can loosen, especially if the crankarm bolts weren't tight to begin with. If you ride with loose crankarms, you'll eventually ruin them. Most crankarm bolts are 14 or 15 millimeters. Get the right size for your crankarms.

Instead of regular bolts, some crankarms use an allen bolt. If yours takes an allen bolt, all you'll need to tighten your crankarms is the right size of allen wrench.

Rear brake cable. Once a cable starts to fray, it usually is not long before it breaks. A brake cable is easy to replace and such a pain to live without. Bring a rear brake cable; it's longer than the front cable, so you can cut it down to use as a front brake cable if you need to.

Rear derailleur cable. This cable is easy to replace and such a pain to live without. It is light and takes up very little space. Bring a rear derailleur cable; it's longer than the front cable, so you can cut it down to use as a front derailleur cable if you need to.

Extra spokes. There are many ways to break a spoke—a crash, a stick in the spokes, the chain overshifting, a big pothole or rock, or, worst of all, a torn-off rear derailleur caught in the spokes. Bring 3 spokes for the front and 9 for the rear: 6 for the freewheel side and 3 for the opposite side.

Spokes come in different lengths. The length of the spokes depends on the brand and model of the hub and rim, on the lacing pattern, and on whether the wheel used is the front or rear. The spokes in a front wheel are all one length; rear spokes are two lengths (the ones on the freewheel side are shorter, the ones on the opposite side are longer). When you go to your local bike shop to purchase spokes, either bring your wheels (they will measure your spokes for you), or tell them the hub and rim brand and model and the lacing pattern. Use a pen and a piece of masking tape to label each set of spokes that you take on the trail with you so that you know which ones go where.

Toe strap. If your pedals are the regular toe clip–and-strap type (that is, not clipless pedals), bring a spare strap to replace a broken toe strap. A toe strap also can be used to temporarily fix a broken freewheel, to hold together a broken seat, or to help splint a broken handlebar.

Rear derailleur. The rear derailleur is in a very vulnerable position and there are plenty of bad things that can happen to it. A root can catch it or you can fall on it, bending or breaking it. Consider taking an extra derailleur on long trips. If you have index shifting, get a derailleur that is compatible with your shifting system.

Freewheel tool or cassette tool. A freewheel tool is used to remove the freewheel from the hub. Different brands and models of freewheels may require different freewheel tools— be sure that you get the right tool for your freewheel.

There are two types of freewheel mechanisms. Before you try to fix a freewheel or freehub, you need to know which type you have.

Standard freewheels have the ratcheting mechanism (the part that lets you stop pedaling and coast) and cogs together as a single part. A standard freewheel is threaded, and screws directly onto the hub.

Freehubs or cassette hubs have the ratcheting mechanism in a freehub body, which is splined on the outside. The freehub body is threaded and screws onto the hub. The cogs slide onto the freehub body. A lockring holds the cogs to the freehub body.

How do you tell the difference? Most older bikes (pre-1990) and many lower-end bikes have freewheels. Most Shimano hubs are freehubs (especially those hubs produced in the 1990s). Later-model Campagnolo and Suntour hubs also have freehubs. If you look at enough wheels, you can recognize them by sight (but who has the time?). If you're not sure, bring your bike to a bike shop and ask. While you're there, ask about the parts and tools you'll need to take with you to replace the freehub body.

Spare tire. Bringing a spare tire may seem like overkill, but it's a lot easier and safer to replace a tire than it is to boot it. If you get a sidewall blowout that is too large to boot, the only solution is to replace it with a new tire. A tire with a Kevlar bead can be folded to about the size of a small water bottle.

Spare freewheel. When you break a freewheel, you can't really fix it, although you can do some things so that you can ride home (see Broken Freewheel, in the Troubleshooting chapter). However, you can easily "fix" a broken freewheel by replacing it with a new one.

If your bike uses a cassette system, the actual "freewheel" mechanism is part of the hub and the cogs slide onto the freehub body. You need a special tool to remove the freehub body, usually a 10-millimeter allen key. To repair a cassette system, instead of just a wrench, a freewheel tool, and an extra freewheel, you will need a tool to remove the cogs, a tool to remove the freewheel mechanism, a wrench, and an extra freehub body.

Cone wrenches. Cone wrenches are used to adjust the bearings in hubs. On rough terrain, the cones in your hubs may loosen slightly, producing lateral play in the wheel. Different models of hubs may take different sizes of cone wrenches; make sure that you get the right size of cone wrenches for your hubs. Normally, the front and rear hubs require different sizes of wrenches. If the locknuts for the cones also have slotted flats, you may also need another cone wrench for the locknut, although most cone locknuts can be turned using an adjustable wrench. Cones for front hubs normally take 13- or 14-millimeter cone wrenches. Rear hub cones normally take 14-, 15-, 16-, or 17-millimeter cone wrenches. You may need up to four cone wrenches to adjust both the front and rear hubs.

Two headset wrenches. A headset wrench is used to adjust the headset bearings. One is used for the locknut and the other for the adjusting race. On rough terrain, the headset may loosen or tighten, affecting steering and stability. Different brands and models of headsets may use different sizes of headset wrenches; make sure that you get the right size of wrench. The most common size is 32 millimeters. If you choose to carry a headset wrench, select one of the small, alloy portable types rather than the large, steel shop types. If you have an Aheadset, you only need the right size allen wrench to adjust the headset.

Bottom bracket wrench. Most conventional bottom brackets are adjusted and secured using a lockring. If you have this type, bring a lockring wrench. This type of bottom bracket also has a fixed cup, which can be tightened with a large bottom bracket wrench. Normally, the factory or bike shop mechanic puts the fixed cup on pretty tight and you shouldn't have to worry about it.

If you choose to carry a lockring or bottom bracket wrench, select one of the small, alloy portable types rather than the large, steel shop types.

Some sealed-bearing bottom brackets may use snap-rings or have their own type of attachment mechanism. They may require special tools, such as a snap-ring tool or a special wrench. Ask a bike mechanic if you're unsure what type you own.

Lubricant. A bicycle chain lubricant can eliminate squeaks in a chain, help loosen tight bolts, and lubricate rough-working parts. Get a lubricant that comes in a squeeze bottle—it's easier to control the flow and placement of the lube.

Spoke wrench. A spoke wrench is used to adjust the tension of your spokes. By adjusting spoke tension, you can straighten slight bends in a rim. Spoke wrenches are small and worth carrying. Spoke nipples come in different sizes; make sure that you get the right size of spoke wrench for your spokes (and for the replacement spokes that you carry with you).

Zip ties. Zip ties are so strong that cops use them as econo-handcuffs for prisoners. You can use them as extra chain links, temporary fixes for broken freewheels, and substitute bolts for loose fenders and racks. You also can use them to hold a seat on a seat post. You should carry small, thin ones (like the ones used to secure cycle computers), medium-sized ones, and large ones. They're light, plastic, and don't take up much space—there's no excuse not to have them.

Pliers. A set of needle-nosed pliers (with wirecutters) can be used to bend chain plates, hold cables while you tighten them, cut cables, and act as a very primitive wrench. If you're into on-trail dentistry, you can use them to pull teeth.

Extra bits and pieces. There are quite a few nuts, bolts, and pieces on your bike that are small and hardly noticeable but are hell to do without or have broken. Here's a list of bits and pieces you'll want to carry with you.

- Crankarm bolts (make sure that you get the right size)
- Chainring bolts
- Spare axles (one front, one rear)
- Seat bolt
- Extra cleats and cleat screws for your shoes
- Extra bearings

Tools for Different Trail Conditions

Sometimes the climate or terrain in which you plan to ride may dictate that you bring special equipment or tools. You also may need to make special preparations to your bike before you ride. The best way to find out the particulars of riding in an area is to ask the locals or a bike shop near the area of your ride.

For example, the Pacific Northwest often is wet and has sandy and abrasive soil. If you plan a long trip in the Pacific Northwest or any place with a similar climate, consider making the following preparations:

- Make sure that you don't start your ride with worn brake pads. Bring an extra set of pads if your trip is going to take longer than a day. The abrasive soil will make the brake pads wear faster—especially in the rain.
- Lube your chain with the stickiest lube you can find so that you don't wash off all your chain lube in the first mud puddle.

◆ Make sure that your cables are greased—on a rainy day or a wet trail, insidious mud and grit will work itself into your cable housing and make it harder to shift gears.

Here are some other common trail conditions and how to prepare for them:

◆ If you think you'll encounter large rocks on the trail, bring extra tubes. The chances of getting a pinch flat increase when you ride on the hard, irregular surfaces of a rocky trail.

◆ If you plan to bike in desertlike conditions you may have to contend with thorns and dust. Be prepared with tire liners or belted tires, and bring extra tubes and patches. Use a light lubricant on your chain, or wax it—a thick or sticky oil attracts dirt and sand and will wear out your chain and freewheel faster.

Carrying It All

Once you've collected all the tools you want to take with you, you need a way to carry them. You can use a seat pack, pannier, or fanny pack. Most people are more comfortable carrying things on their bikes than on their backs. No matter what you choose as your carrying pack, follow these tips to protect your tools and keep them from rattling:

◆ Wrap a rag such as a small towel or shop rag around the tools to keep the tools from rattling and to use to wipe your hands.

◆ Close the rag by wrapping duct tape around it; this will keep the rag in place and keep extra duct tape handy for repairs.

◆ Pack the tools in a self-sealing plastic bag to keep them dry; you can use the plastic bag as an emergency boot for a ripped sidewall.

TROUBLESHOOTING

Bottom Bracket

LOOSE BOTTOM BRACKET

Diagnosis ♦ The bottom bracket has play. To check for a loose bottom bracket, grab the crankarms and try moving the crankarms side to side. If you can feel any internal movement or a knock when you move the crankarms to each side, the bottom bracket is loose. A loose bottom bracket can cause poor front derailleur shifting.

Emergency repair ♦ If you have a conventional bottom bracket (that is, it has a notched lockring) and you don't have a bottom bracket wrench, use a flat head screwdriver to loosen or tighten the lockring. Place the flat of the screwdriver in one of the notches of the lockring on the side of the notch. Get a rock and hit the handle of the screwdriver so that the lockring turns (use the rock and screwdriver like a hammer and chisel, but instead of chiseling, you'll be using the force of the screwdriver flat to turn the lockring). You also can use the screwdriver-and-rock technique to turn the adjustable cup. Using these techniques instead of the correct tools, adjust the bottom bracket by following the steps in Adjusting a Bottom Bracket, in the Real Repairs chapter.

If you don't have any tools, you can ride with the bottom bracket loose.

Permanent repair ◆ Adjust the bottom bracket (see Adjusting a Bottom Bracket, in the Real Repairs chapter).

TIGHT OR SEIZED BOTTOM BRACKET

Diagnosis ◆ The crankarm does not turn smoothly. A tight bottom bracket can be caused by damaged bearings (or races) or by poor adjustment.

Other parts of the drive train could be causing the extra resistance; make sure that the brake pads are not rubbing and that the rear wheel is mounted correctly and is not rubbing against the chainstays. To check if the bottom bracket is really the problem, remove the chain from the chainring and rest the chain on the bottom bracket shell. Turn the crankarms to see if they turn freely. If there is resistance or the crankarm doesn't turn, the bottom bracket is causing the problem.

Emergency repair and permanent repair ◆ Adjust the bottom bracket (see Sealed Bottom Bracket, in the Real Repairs chapter).

If you can't get the bottom bracket into proper adjustment, it may be damaged. When you get back from your ride, check the bottom bracket's bearings and bearing surfaces. If the bottom bracket is worn or damaged, replace it.

Brakes and Brake Levers

BRAKE PADS RUB AGAINST RIM

Diagnosis ◆ One or both brake pads rub against the rim.

If a brake pad rubs non-stop against the rim, the wheel may not be aligned correctly in the dropouts, the centering of the brakes may need adjustment, or the rim may be bent.

Emergency repair and permanent repair ✦ If the wheel isn't squarely centered in the dropouts, remount the wheel correctly (see Removing and Installing a Wheel, in the Real Repairs chapter) and check the brake adjustment (see Centering Cantilever Brakes, U-Brakes, and Power Cams, in the Real Repairs chapter). If the rim is bent, true the wheel (see Truing a Wheel, in the Real Repairs chapter) and then recheck the brake adjustment.

If these things are OK, center the brakes (see Centering Cantilever Brakes, U-Brakes, and Power Cams, in the Real Repairs chapter).

BRAKE PADS RUB AGAINST TIRE OR SLIDE OFF RIM

Diagnosis ✦ The brake pads rub against the casing of the tire, or the brake pads slip and dive off the rim (the brake pads may even get stuck beneath the rim). The height or angle of the brake pads is out of adjustment. This can be caused by poor brake adjustment or worn brake pads.

Check the brake pads for wear. Most brake pads have grooves or marks molded into the braking surface or the top of the pad. When these grooves are worn off or the pad has worn past the marks, the brake pad is worn out. If your brake pads don't have any marks, you can use this rule of thumb. Most brake pads are about ½ of an inch thick. If the pad is worn down ¼ of an inch or more, it is worn out and should be replaced.

Emergency repair and permanent repair ✦ If you have a 10-millimeter wrench and a small adjustable wrench, see Adjusting a Brake Pad, in the Real Repairs chapter. If you don't have these wrenches, there is nothing you can do.

BRAKES STICK

Diagnosis ✦ The brake lever does not return at all when you release it or it returns sluggishly. You also may feel some binding when you pull the brake lever. There are three common causes for this: the cable is dry (unlubricated) or rusty; the cable is frayed; or the cable is dirty or gritty (this is common on muddy trails).

Occasionally, a broken or weak spring in the cantilever brake will cause the brake pads to drag or cause the brake lever to return sluggishly. If this seems to be the cause, see the section Broken Cantilever Spring in this chapter.

A heavily worn rim also can cause some sticking. The brake pads may have worn a small groove or channel in the rim. The brake pad can get temporarily hung up on the ridge of the groove, causing the brakes to stick or the lever to return slowly. Try using the sandpaper in your patch kit to smooth the ridge of the groove so the brake pad doesn't hang up.

If the cable is dry or dirty, clean it and lubricate it with grease or oil if you have it with you.

If the cable is frayed, replace it (see Replacing a Brake Cable, in the Real Repairs chapter).

BRAKES SQUEAL

Diagnosis ◆ Brakes make a squealing sound. Make sure that the brake pads are properly adjusted. Usually, squealing occurs when the brake pads aren't toed in properly.

A dirty rim also can cause noisy braking. The rim may have a layer of grit, dirt, mud, oil, or brake pad residue. The rim also may have a finish that causes the noise.

If you have new brake pads, the composition of brake pad material may cause squeaking. Some brake pads have a finish on the surface. Usually after you wear the pad down a little, the roughened surface of the brake pad enables it to grip the rim better, making the noise go away.

Emergency repair and permanent repair ◆ If the rim is dirty, try wiping it clean.

Check the surfaces of the brake pads (especially if you have new brake pads). If there is a layer of lacquer or other compound on the surface of the pad, use the sandpaper from your patch kit to roughen it.

If none of this works, adjust the brake pads (see Adjusting Brake Pads, in the Real Repairs chapter).

Some brake pads are evil by nature and will refuse to stop squealing no matter what you do. These must be replaced (unless you like the noise).

LITTLE OR NO BRAKING POWER

Diagnosis ◆ Four things can cause you to lose braking power.

Worn brake pads. Check the brake pads for wear. Most brake pads have grooves or marks molded into the braking surface or the top of pad. When these grooves are worn off or the pad has worn past the marks, the brake pad is worn out. If your brake pads don't have any marks, you can use this rule of thumb: since most brake pads are about ½ of an inch thick, if the pad is worn down a ¼ of an inch or more, it is worn out and should be replaced.

Stretched brake cable. If the clearance between the brake pad and rim is more than ½ of an inch, adjust the cable tension on your brakes—you probably already noticed you don't have much braking power. (See Adjusting Brake Cable Tension, in the Real Repairs chapter.)

Poor grip between brake pads and rim. No matter how hard you pull the brake lever, you don't get any braking power. The surface of the rim or of the brake pad may be coated with grime or have a finish that doesn't allow the brake pad to grab the rim. See the sections Brakes Stick and Brakes Squeal.

Poor contact between brake pads and rim. When you pull on the brake lever, the brake pads dive off the rim or rub the tire. See Brake Pads Rub Against Tire or Slide Off Rim.

Emergency repair and permanent repair ◆ For worn brake pads, replace them if you have a spare set. Otherwise, adjust the cable tension (see Adjusting Brake Cable Tension, in the Real Repairs chapter).

For a stretched brake cable, adjust the brake cable tension.

BROKEN CANTILEVER SPRING

Diagnosis ◆ The brake pad drags against the rim (doesn't release from the rim when you release the brake lever). Additionally, the brake lever may not return at all when you release it or may return sluggishly.

Make sure that the wheel is installed correctly. Make sure that the brakes are not simply out of adjustment.

Emergency repair ◆ Try removing the cantilever spring from the cantilever opposite the side that is dragging so that it doesn't pull that side against the rim. The brake will still drag on the rim but not as much as it would with one good cantilever spring and one bad one.

Permanent repair ◆ Replace the spring.

BROKEN BRAKE LEVER

Diagnosis ◆ Brake lever is broken.

Emergency repair ◆ If the tip of the lever is broken off, wrap a piece of duct tape around the end so that the sharp edge doesn't impale you if you crash. If the brake lever breaks at the joint, the only thing you can do is replace the lever.

Permanent repair ◆ Replace the brake lever.

Crankarms and Pedals

LOOSE CRANKARM

Diagnosis ◆ Crankarm is loose on the bottom bracket spindle. A loose crankarm can affect shifting or cause the chainrings to rub on the frame or front derailleur.

Check to see if the crankarm hole is rounded. If it is rounded, see the section Rounded Crankarm Hole.

Emergency repair and permanent repair ◆ The crankarm bolt needs to be tightened. Use a crankarm wrench to tighten the crankarm bolt. If you don't have a crankarm wrench, try using a flat head screwdriver to turn the crankarm bolt. You can use a rock as a hammer and the screwdriver as a punch.

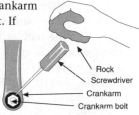

Rock
Screwdriver
Crankarm
Crankarm bolt

If you've lost your crankarm bolt, mount the crankarm and use a small log or stick to pound the crankarm until it is tight on the spindle. You may want to carry the log or stick with you so you can pound on the crankarm if it comes loose again.

CRANKARM HAS FALLEN OFF

Diagnosis ◆ The crankarm has fallen off of the bottom bracket spindle.

Look at the bottom bracket spindle to see if your crankarm is attached with a bolt or nut. If the crankarm attaches with a bolt, the end of the spindle will have a threaded hole where the crankarm bolt screws in. If the crankarm attaches with a nut, the end of the spindle will have a threaded end where the nut screws on. If you have single-key release crankarms, you'll see an allen bolt head on the crankarm.

If you don't have single-key release crankarms, you need to find the crankarm bolt or nut. If you have a dust cap on the crankarm, the dust cap will have retained the bolt or nut. Unscrew the dust cap and retrieve the bolt or nut. If you have a bolt, it usually has a washer with it (the washer prevents the hard steel bolt from grinding into the soft aluminum crank).

If you've lost your attachment bolt, try to find it.

Emergency repair and permanent repair • Reattach the crank.

If you don't have a crankarm wrench and/or you've lost your attachment bolt or nut, install your crankarm using the emergency tightening techniques in Loose Crankarm.

If you have found your crankarm nut or bolt, clean the surface of the bottom bracket spindle (grit or dirt on the spindle can cause creaking). If the right side crank has fallen off, untangle the chain, shift the front derailleur to the small chainring, and reinstall the chain on the small chainring. Place the crankarm on the bottom bracket spindle. Make sure that the crankarm is in the right position—the crankarms should be pointing in opposite directions. Reinstall the crankarm bolt or nut; be sure it's tight.

ROUNDED CRANKARM HOLE

Diagnosis • The crankarm won't stay tightened; the crankarm is loose on the bottom bracket spindle when the crankarm bolt is tightened as much as possible; the crankarm bolt bottoms out on the bottom bracket spindle (instead of on the crankarm); or you lost the crankarm bolt or nut. The crankarm hole is usually square or octagonal. If the crankarm has been loose for an extended period of time, the hole may become rounded or severely indented by the spindle.

Emergency repair • To make the crankarm fit tighter, shim the rounded hole with pieces of metal.

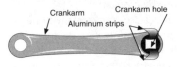

Crankarm
Crankarm hole
Aluminum strips

Find an aluminum can. Cut or tear small strips of aluminum to use to shim the tapered end of the bottom bracket spindle. Wrap a small strip around the spindle taper (a little aluminum goes a long way). As a substitute, you can use a piece of derailleur cable. Use wire cutters or pliers to cut off some of the extra cable from your derailleur cable. Thread the derailleur cable through the crankarm hole; the cable will flatten when you tighten the crank. Install the crankarm on the shimmed taper. Make sure that the crankarm is tight (doesn't wobble on the spindle). If it is still loose, add more aluminum strips or cable.

If you don't have a bolt and you don't have anything to use as a shim, find a small log (or a rock if you don't value your crankarm very much) and pound the crankarm back on. Note that if you use this technique, you risk permanently damaging your crankarm.

Permanent repair ◆ Replace the crankarm or use steel shims.

BENT CRANKARM

Diagnosis ◆ Crankarm is bent. A bent crankarm can affect your pedaling motion (it may feel like the pedal axle is bent) or cause the crankarm to rub against the chainstay.

Emergency repair and permanent repair ◆ You can try to bend the crankarm straight.

Before you start bending, check the crankarm for cracks. If the crankarm is cracked, you'll probably break it when you try to bend it straight. Leave it alone and ride home (unless it's unrideable—in which case, you're stuck walking the bike). Avoid putting all of your weight on the cracked crankarm. Replace it when you get home.

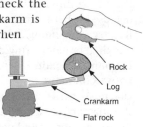

Rock

Log

Crankarm

Flat rock

If the crankarm isn't cracked, turn it so that the bent crankarm is pointing toward the ground. Find a flat rock to support the crankarm (about 5 inches thick), a big rock to pound the crankarm straight, and a piece of wood to protect the crankarm from direct impact with the rock. Lay the bike on the ground with the bent crankarm side down. Slide the flat rock beneath the crankarm near the crankarm bolt so that it supports the crankarm. Use the piece of wood to disperse the impact on the crankarm by placing it at the pedal-end of the crankarm. Pound on the piece of wood with the other rock until the crankarm is straight; be sure not to bend the crankarm too far).

If you can't find rocks but you do have a friend, place a solid piece of wood or other hard object beneath the crankarm bolt, have your friend hold the bike steady, and bend the crankarm by standing on it. Don't put all of your weight on the crank—use just enough weight to bend the crankarm straight.

LOST CHAINRING BOLTS

Diagnosis ◆ One or more chainring nut-and-bolt sets (holds the chainrings to the crankarm) is missing.

Emergency repair ◆ If you carried along some zip ties, use one to help secure the chainrings to the crankarm. Thread the zip tie through the chainring hole (where the nut and bolt used to be) and tighten the zip tie. As a desperate alternative, try substituting a stick for a chainring bolt by screwing, wedging, or hammering the stick into the bolt hole.

Permanent repair ◆ Replace the bolt.

LOOSE CHAINRING

Diagnosis ◆ The chainring bolts are loose. This can cause poor shifting or create a rattling noise.

Emergency repair and permanent repair ◆ Tighten the loose bolts. If you've lost your chainring bolts, replace them or, if you don't have extras, see the solution in the section Lost Chainring Bolts.

BENT BIG CHAINRING

Diagnosis ◆ The body of the outer chainring is bent or its teeth are bent. A bent chainring can cause poor shifting (chain may fall off when you shift to the large chainring) or cause the chainring to rub against the front derailleur (you may hear the chain scraping against the front derailleur at a regular interval). A bent chainring can be caused by an object hitting the chainring (bumping it against a rock or a log while riding, for example) or poor front derailleur adjustment (front derailleur may be mounted too low or it may be bent). See the section Chain Falls Off Big Chainring.

Emergency repair ◆ Find the bends in the chainring body or teeth. To do this, shift the chain to the middle or small chainring, turn the crankarms backward, and watch the large chainring. If the chainring or any of its teeth wobble back and forth laterally, that's where it's bent. Use an adjustable wrench to bend the bent teeth or bent areas of the chainring straight so that the lateral wobble in the chainring is eliminated, or at least until the bend no longer affects shifting.

If just the chainring body is bent, use a rock to pound the chainring straight. If the chainring is bent to the inside, use the straightening technique outlined in the section, Bent Small Chainring.

Permanent repair ◆ If you weren't able to straighten the chainring completely while out on the trail, remove the chainring and continue to flatten it out with a hammer or a vise. If the chainring cannot be straightened, replace it.

BENT SMALL CHAINRING

Diagnosis ◆ The inner chainring body is bent or its teeth are bent.

A bent chainring can cause poor shifting (the chain may fall off when you shift to the small chainring). A bent chainring can be caused by a jammed chain that resulted from poor front derailleur adjustment (the front derailleur may overshift causing the chain to be jammed between the small chainring and chainstay; this type of chain jamming usually bends the chainring). See the section Chain Falls Off Small Chainring.

Emergency repair ✦ Find the bends in the chainring or teeth. To find bends in the chainring, shift the chain to the large chainring, turn the crankarms backward, and watch the small chainring carefully. If the chainring or any of its teeth wobble back and forth laterally, the chainring or teeth are bent. Use a screwdriver to bend the bent teeth or to pry the bent areas of the chainring straight so that the lateral wobble in the chainring is eliminated, or at least until the bend no longer affects shifting.

If just the chainring body is bent, use a rock and a flathead screwdriver to pound the chainring straight. Place the end of the screwdriver on the bend. Pound the end of the screwdriver with a rock until the chainring is straight. If you don't have a screwdriver, try using an allen key.

Permanent repair ✦ If you weren't able to straighten the chainring completely while on the trail, remove the chainring and continue to flatten it out with a hammer or a vise. If the chainring cannot be straightened, replace it.

BROKEN PEDAL CAGE

Diagnosis ✦ Cage of the pedal has fallen off or is severely bent.

Emergency repair ✦ If the cage is severely bent and the cage is still attached to the pedal, leave it alone if the pedal still rotates on the axle. If you have clipless pedals, don't clip into that pedal and you can pedal with the middle or heel of your foot. However, the pedal will be frozen on the pedal axle so that the body of the pedal will rotate as you pedal (the pedal would normally spin on the pedal axle). Let the pedal rotate under your foot. If you have toe clips and straps, remove them from the pedal and you can continue pedaling. Let the pedal rotate under your foot. If you have a cleat on your shoe, don't let it engage in the pedal.

If the cage has fallen off and you have no bolts but do have zip ties, try this trick. A regular pedal (non-clipless) mounts onto a body. The body usually has rectangular holes that the toe strap goes through to secure it to the body and the cage; the cage should also have holes. Attach the cage to the pedal body using zip ties; thread the zip ties through the holes in the cage and body.

Permanent repair ◆ Replace the cage or pedal.

CAN'T RELEASE SHOE FROM A SHIMANO SPD PEDAL

Diagnosis ◆ A shoe is stuck in the pedal. The cleat is loose or worn, or the clipping mechanism is jammed with debris.

Emergency repair ◆ To escape from the pedal, take your foot out of the shoe. Try to turn the shoe to see if the clipping mechanism disengages. If it does, hold it in that position. If it doesn't, try loosening the tension adjustment bolt on the pedal (usually an allen head bolt at the back of the pedal). Use a flathead screwdriver to further disengage the plate that holds the clipping mechanism. Try turning the shoe to release it. If the shoe doesn't release, ride with the straps of the shoe loose so that you can pull your foot out of the shoe if necessary.

Permanent repair ◆ Tighten your cleats, or, if that doesn't solve the problem, install new ones.

frame and fork

BENT FORK

Diagnosis ◆ Fork is bent. Usually, a fork will bend, crack, or break only during a crash. Follow the inspection tips in Inspecting Your Bike After a Crash, in the Before You Hit the Trail chapter.

If there are any bends or cracks in the fork, it must be replaced. Avoid riding with a damaged fork (think of riding along and then having someone suddenly take your front wheel away). If you choose to ride, do it at a pace at which you would feel comfortable falling down.

BENT OR BROKEN FRAME

Diagnosis ◆ Usually, a frame will bend, crack, or break only during a crash. However, a frame can crack or break from metal fatigue or defect. If your bike creaks or clicks and you can't find any other problems (such as a loose bottom bracket, loose crankarm, loose chainrings, and so on), the frame could be cracked.

Follow the inspection tips in Inspecting Your Bike After a Crash, in the Before You Hit the Trail chapter. Cracks are dangerous because they usually get larger from the stress of riding. If you choose to ride with a cracked frame, check the crack periodically to make sure that it is not getting bigger.

A severe bend, break, or crack can affect the handling and structural integrity of the bike. You probably should walk the bike, but if you choose to ride, ride very slowly and carefully and dismount for steep descents.

Emergency repair ◆ If the break or crack is in the middle of the tube, use strong sticks or your pump as splints and duct tape to hold the splints in place. If you choose to ride using this makeshift repair, ride very slowly and carefully—avoid steep descents (dismount) and big bumps and potholes. If the break or crack is at a joint, don't ride the bike.

Permanent repair ◆ Regardless of the size of a dent, bend, or crack, have your frame checked and repaired at a bike shop that also offers a frameshop or by a custom framebuilder.

Headsets

LOOSE HEADSET

Diagnosis ✦ Headset has play. A loose headset can cause the bike to have unstable handling, or cause rattling noises when riding over rough terrain. A loose headset eventually will ruin the headset and possibly bend the steerer tube of the fork. If you can't fix it on the trail, be sure to fix it when you get home.

To check for a loose headset, hold the front brake so that the front wheel is locked and move the bike forward and back. If you can feel any internal movement (make sure that it's not the brake that's moving) or you feel a knock when you move the bike, the headset is loose.

If you have front suspension, you won't be able to do this test. Instead, lift the front wheel off the ground and try moving the fork side to side. If you feel internal movement or a knock, the headset is loose.

Emergency repair ✦ If you don't have a wrench that will fit the headset locknut, you won't be able to do much to fix it. Try turning the locknut and top bearing cup by hand to tighten the headset. The headset will work its way loose again, so be ready to hand-tighten it again.

Permanent repair ✦ Adjust the headset (see Adjusting a Headset, in the Real Repairs chapter).

TIGHT HEADSET

Diagnosis ✦ Headset binds continuously or settles into one spot. A tight headset prevents the handlebar from freely turning side to side.

Check to make sure the problem isn't caused by brake or derailleur cables caught or tangled on something. A tight headset can be caused by damaged bearings (or bearing surfaces) in the headset, by a bent steerer tube, or by poor adjustment.

Emergency repair ◆ If you don't have a wrench that will fit the headset locknut, you won't be able to fix the problem.

Permanent repair ◆ Adjust the headset (see Adjusting a Headset, in the Real Repairs chapter).

If you can't get the headset into proper adjustment, the headset may be damaged. When you get back from your ride, check the headset's bearings and bearing surfaces. If the headset is worn or damaged, replace it. If the headset is in good shape, bring your fork to a frame shop to check for a bent steerer tube.

CRACKED HEADSET

Diagnosis ◆ One or both cups on the headset are cracked.

Emergency repair ◆ Leave it alone. Do not try to tighten the headset (tightening the headset will only make the crack larger).

Permanent repair ◆ Replace the headset.

Shifters, Derailleurs, and Chains

INDEX SHIFTING SKIPS OR DOESN'T SHIFT (REAR DERAILLEUR)

Diagnosis ◆ When you shift one gear with the shift lever, the chain does not shift to the next gear or the chain skips between the two gears (that is, it doesn't shift completely to the next gear). Usually, poor index shifting is caused by a stretched cable. Cables, particularly new ones, will stretch and seat in with use, so you normally can fix your index shifting problems by adjusting the cable tension.

Poor indexing also can be caused by a loose cable attachment bolt, a frayed derailleur cable, a bent rear derailleur hanger, or a worn chain or freewheel.

If the chain skips at a regular interval even with the shifting adjusted correctly, the chain probably has a tight link. See the section Chain Has a Tight Link.

Emergency repair ◆ If you don't have any tools and your shifter has a friction mode, switch the shifter to friction mode. You won't get index shifting but you'll at least be able to move the shifter around so that you can find each gear. If you don't have a friction mode, try adjusting the rear derailleur; see Adjusting Index Shifting (Rear Derailleur), in the Real Repairs chapter. If adjusting the shifting for the rear derailleur doesn't solve the problem, check the following things:

Check for a loose cable attachment bolt. If this bolt is loose, follow these steps to tighten the cable:

1. Shift the rear derailleur to the smallest cog.
2. Loosen the bolt so you can adjust the cable tension.
3. Pull the cable so that there is no slack in the cable (however, make sure that the cable is not so tight that it moves the rear derailleur).
4. Hold the cable and tighten the cable adjustment bolt.
5. Adjust the index shifting; see Adjusting Index Shifting (Rear Derailleur), in the Real Repairs chapter.

Check for a frayed derailleur cable. Replace the cable (see Replacing a Derailleur Cable, in the Real Repairs chapter). If you don't have a spare, see the emergency repair in the section Broken Derailleur Cable.

Check the rear derailleur for damage. For information about checking for damage and repairing it, see the sections Bent Rear Derailleur and Broken Rear Derailleur Pulley.

Check for a worn freewheel or chain. For information about checking for a worn freewheel, see the section Chain Skips.

Permanent repair ◆ Adjust the index shifting; see Adjusting Index Shifting (Rear Derailleur), in the Real Repairs chapter.

INDEX SHIFTING DOESN'T SHIFT OR CHAIN RUBS (FRONT DERAILLEUR)

Diagnosis • When you shift one click with the shift lever, the chain does not shift at all to the next chainring or the chain skips between the two chainrings (that is, it does not shift completely to the next chainring). Usually, poor index shifting is caused by a stretched cable. Cables will stretch and seat in with use (particularly new ones). So you can normally fix your index shifting problems by adjusting the cable tension.

Poor indexing on the front derailleur can also be caused by a loose cable attachment bolt, a frayed derailleur cable, a bent front derailleur cage, an improperly mounted front derailleur, or a worn chain.

If the chain skips at a regular interval, even with the shifting adjusted correctly, the chain probably has a tight link (see the section Chain Has a Tight Link).

If front index shifting is out of adjustment, the chain may also rub on the front derailleur cage. Normally, you should get little or no chain rub with the chain on the middle chainring when shifting through all the gears on the rear derailleur. When you have the chain on the big chainring, you may get some rubbing with the rear derailleur shifted to the larger cogs on the freewheel—this is normal. You may also get some rubbing when the chain is in the small chainring/small rear cog combination—this is also normal. However, you need to adjust the front derailleur if the chain rubs against the front derailleur in the large chainring/small cog or small chainring/large cog combination (see the section Adjusting a Front Derailleur, in the Real Repairs chapter).

Emergency repair • If you don't have any tools and your shifter has a friction mode, switch the shifter to friction mode.

You won't get index shifting, but you'll at least be able to move the shifter around so that you can find the exact position of each gear.

Permanent repair ◆ If the front derailleur is mounted incorrectly, move the shifter to the lowest gear (small chainring) and release the front derailleur cable by loosening the cable attachment bolt. Loosen the front derailleur mounting bolt. Turn the front derailleur so that the front derailleur cage aligns with the chainrings (the front part of the cage should be parallel with the chainrings). Tighten the mounting bolt; re-attach the front derailleur cable; adjust the front derailleur (see Adjusting a Front Derailleur, in the Real Repairs chapter).

Also check the vertical position of the front derailleur. To check for the correct front derailleur height, shift to the middle chainring and then use your hand to push the front derailleur cage so that the outside cage is directly over the teeth of the large chainring. There should be ⅛ to ½ of an inch of clearance between the outside cage and the large chainring. If the outside cage of the front derailleur rubs against the teeth on the large chainring, the front derailleur is undoubtedly mounted too low. To adjust the height of the front derailleur, shift the front derailleur to the small chainring and release the front derailleur cable by loosening the cable attachment bolt. Loosen the front derailleur mounting bolt. Raise or lower the front derailleur. Tighten the mounting bolt. Check the front derailleur height. Move the derailleur again if necessary. Check the derailleur's lateral adjustment (make sure that the front part of the derailleur cage is parallel to the chainrings). Reattach the front derailleur cable.

If the front derailleur is mounted correctly, try adjusting the index shifting for the front derailleur; see Adjusting Index Shifting (Front Derailleur), in the Real Repairs chapter.

BENT REAR DERAILLEUR CAGE OR DERAILLEUR HANGER

Diagnosis ◆ The derailleur's cage is bent. The bent derailleur cage may rub against the spokes or cause poor shifting.

From the rear of the bike, check the derailleur cage. If the cage is not parallel to the cogs, the cage probably is bent. Make sure that the derailleur hanger is straight; a bent derailleur hanger may make the derailleur look as if it is bent. If the derailleur is cracked or twisted beyond hope, follow the steps in the section Broken Rear Derailleur.

Emergency repair ◆ If the derailleur cage is only bent (not cracked or twisted), you can bend it straight. Start by shifting the rear derailleur to the smallest cog. The derailleur must be on the smallest cog (this is the end of the derailleur's range of shifting motion) so that you'll be bending the derailleur instead of moving the derailleur. Put the bike on its side with the derailleur side up. Put one palm against the derailleur hanger bolt to prevent the derailleur hanger from bending and to stabilize the bike. Grab the derailleur cage near the lower pulley wheel and pull it until it is straight. Don't go too far—derailleur cages made of aluminum may fatigue and crack if bent back and forth too severely or too many times. Check the cage's alignment with the cogs. Bend the cage again if necessary. When the cage is straight or nearly straight, try shifting the derailleur to the large cog and then the small cog. If the derailleur doesn't shift to these cogs, adjust the derailleur (see Adjusting the Rear Derailleur, in the Real Repairs chapter). Adjust the index shifting if necessary (see Adjusting Index Shifting, in the Real Repairs chapter).

Permanent repair ◆ If the bend in the derailleur cage is not very severe (that is, you can bend it straight), you probably don't need to replace the derailleur. However, you should check the derailleur for further damage, such as cracks in the derailleur body or cage, when you get back from your ride. You may also want to replace the cage.

Straightening a bent derailleur hanger. If you've straightened the derailleur all you can and shifting is still affected, the derailleur hanger may be bent. Straighten the derailleur hanger with an adjustable wrench. Remove the rear derailleur from the derailleur hanger (loosen the derailleur attachment bolt). Put the wrench on the derailleur hanger and tighten the wrench so that it holds the hanger securely. Bend the derailleur hanger until it is straight. Do not bend the derailleur hanger too far. Reattach the derailleur and check the alignment of the cage. Straighten the hanger again if necessary. If you are still having problems, have a good bike shop align the derailleur hanger. If that doesn't fix the problem, replace the derailleur.

BROKEN REAR DERAILLEUR

Diagnosis ◆ The rear derailleur's body is broken off from the frame or the derailleur's cage is severely bent or broken so that the chain cannot pass freely through the pulley wheels.
Emergency repair ◆ If you have a chain tool, you can turn your bike into a one-speed. Use the chain tool to break the chain. Take out enough links so that the chain can fit the middle chainring in the front and the middle freewheel cog in the back. Reconnect the chain. It's best to have about 1 inch of play in the chain. If the chain has too much slack, it will fall off. If the chain is too tight, it may break.

To get the chain on the cog and chainring, put the chain on the freewheel cog you want to use. Then wrap the chain onto the top teeth of the middle chainring and turn the crank-arms forward; watch your fingers. The chain should ride onto the chainring.

If the cage is destroyed but not bent into the spokes, and

the derailleur is fine, leave the derailleur on the frame.

The derailleur can get tangled in the spokes if the derailleur is broken off of the frame. If you have an allen wrench, you can remove the rear derailleur and its cable. If you don't have an allen wrench, secure the derailleur to the chainstay with a toe strap, duct tape, or shoe string, so that it won't fall into the spokes.

Permanent repair ◆ Replace the derailleur.

BROKEN REAR DERAILLEUR PULLEY WHEELS

Diagnosis ◆ The rear derailleur's pulley wheels have broken teeth or are jammed and won't turn.

Emergency repair ◆ Back in the old days, some types of rear derailleurs didn't have pulley wheels; today, some bike component designers are utilizing this design again. You can, too by taking off the broken pulley wheels, removing the broken pulley wheel body, and reinstalling only the axle of the pulley wheels. If you do this, shifting may be less precise.

Permanent repair ◆ Replace the broken pulley wheels (see Replacing a Broken Pulley Wheel on a Rear Derailleur, in the Real Repairs chapter).

BROKEN DERAILLEUR CABLE

Diagnosis ◆ The derailleur cable is severed.

Emergency repair ◆ If the derailleur cable is broken at the shifter end of the cable and near the very end of the cable, you may have enough extra cable length to tie a knot at the frayed end of the cable. Use pliers if you've got them—the frayed cable strands are sharp! Here's another option: wrap the frayed end around an extra bolt and tighten an extra nut down onto the wrapped cable, creating a makeshift cable-end. Reinstall the renovated cable.

If the derailleur cable is broken in the middle of the cable or near the derailleur end, you can replace or remove the cable.

A broken cable can get tangled in your spokes or brakes and may cause a crash.

If you remove the cable, use the adjustment screws for the derailleur to move the derailleur to the middle cog (rear derailleur) or middle chainring (front derailleur). This will enable you to use a reasonable range of gears, and it will help prevent the chain from coming off.

If the front derailleur cable is broken, place the chain on the middle chainring and use the derailleur's low gear adjusting screw (there are two screws on top of the derailleur; the low gear adjusting screw is the one closest to the bike and is marked L for low) to center the derailleur cage on the middle chainring. You can shift using only the rear derailleur now.

If the rear derailleur cable is broken, move the chain over to one of the middle cogs and use the derailleur's high gear adjusting screw (the screw usually is located above the low gear screw and is marked H for high) to center the derailleur's pulley wheels on the middle cog. You can shift using only the front derailleur now.

Permanent repair • Replace the derailleur cable (see Replacing a Derailleur Cable, in the Real Repairs chapter).

CHAIN FALLS OFF BIG CHAINRING

Diagnosis • When you shift onto the big chainring with the front derailleur, the chain does not stay on the big chainring.

The high gear setting for the front derailleur probably is out of adjustment, the front derailleur cage is bent, or—the least likely possibility—the front derailleur is mounted incorrectly. If you have index shifting on the front derailleur, the index shifting may be out of adjustment.

Emergency repair and permanent repair • If the front derailleur is out of adjustment, adjust it (see Adjusting a Front Derailleur, in the Real Repairs chapter). If you have index shifting, adjust the index shifting; see Adjusting Index Shifting (Front Derailleur), in the Real Repairs chapter.

If the front derailleur cage is bent, bend it straight using pliers, an adjustable wrench, or your hand. The front part of the cage should be parallel with the chainrings.

If the front derailleur is mounted incorrectly, move the shifter to the lowest gear and release the front derailleur cable by loosening the cable attachment bolt. Loosen the front derailleur mounting bolt. Turn the front derailleur so that the front derailleur cage aligns with the chainrings (the front part of the cage should be parallel with the chainrings). Tighten the mounting bolt. Reattach the front derailleur cable. If necessary, adjust the front derailleur. See the section Index Shifting Skips or Doesn't Shift (Rear Derailleur).

CHAIN FALLS OFF SMALL CHAINRING

Diagnosis ◆ When you shift onto the small chainring with the front derailleur, the chain does not stay on the small chainring (never makes it down to the chainring, falls off of the small chainring onto the front derailleur cage, or jams between the bottom bracket and crankarm).

The low gear setting for the front derailleur probably is out of adjustment, the front derailleur cage is bent, or—the least likely possibility—the front derailleur is mounted incorrectly. If you have index shifting on the front derailleur, the index shifting may be out of adjustment.

If the chain jams between the bottom bracket and crankarm, you may also have a bent small chainring (this is especially likely if the chainring is made of aluminum). See the section Bent Small Chainring.

Emergency repair and permanent repair ◆ If the front derailleur is out of adjustment, adjust it (see Adjusting the Front Derailleur, in the Real Repairs chapter). If you have index shifting, adjust the index shifting; see Adjusting Index Shifting

(Front Derailleur), in the Real Repairs chapter.

If the front derailleur cage is bent, bend it straight using pliers, an adjustable wrench, or your hand. The front part of the cage should be parallel to the chainrings.

If the front derailleur is mounted incorrectly, move the shifter to the lowest gear and release the front derailleur cable by loosening the cable attachment bolt. Loosen the front derailleur mounting bolt. Turn the front derailleur so that the front derailleur cage aligns with the chainrings. Tighten the mounting bolt. Reattach the front derailleur cable. Adjust the front derailleur if necessary. See the section Index Shifting Skips or Doesn't Shift (Rear Derailleur).

CHAIN FALLS OFF SMALL COG

Diagnosis ◆ When you shift onto the small cog with the rear derailleur, the chain does not stay on the small cog (never makes it down to the cog or falls off the cog and jams between the freewheel and frame). The high gear setting for the rear derailleur probably is out of adjustment, the rear derailleur cage is bent, or the rear derailleur hanger is bent.

Emergency repair ◆ Switch the shifter to friction mode if you have it. You won't get index-shifting but you'll at least be able to move the shifter around so that you can find the exact position of each gear. If you don't have a friction mode, try adjusting the rear derailleur.

Permanent repair ◆ Adjust the rear derailleur (see Adjusting a Rear Derailleur, in the Real Repairs chapter).

CHAIN FALLS OFF LARGE COG

Diagnosis ◆ When you shift onto the large cog with the rear derailleur, the chain does not stay on the large cog (never makes it up to the cog or falls off the cog and jams between the freewheel and spokes). The low gear setting for the rear derailleur probably is out of adjustment, the rear derailleur cage is bent, or the rear derailleur hanger is bent.

Emergency repair and permanent repair ✦ Adjust the rear derailleur (see Adjusting a Rear Derailleur, in the Real Repairs chapter).

BROKEN CHAIN

Diagnosis ✦ One or more links in the chain are broken.

Emergency repair ✦ If you don't have a chain tool, there are three methods that you can try in order to reassemble a broken chain.

The quick release method. If you're lucky enough to still have the pivot pin for the broken link, use the rear quick release on your wheel to press the pin back in and reconnect the chain. To do this, loosen the quick release; place the chain link with the distended pin between the quick release nut and the dropout; tighten the quick release enough to fully reinsert the pin in the chain. To reinstall the chain, remount the chain (see Installing a Chain, in the Real Repairs chapter) and use the rear quick release to press in the pin.

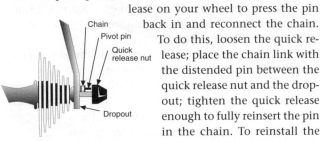

Chain
Pivot pin
Quick release nut
Dropout

The caveman method. Rocks were one of the few tools available to our cave-dwelling ancestors. What's good enough for them is good enough for you.

If the chain plate is bent, hammer it straight using two rocks, one to place the chain on and one to pound with.

If you've lost the pin for the broken link, force the pin next on the chain partially out of the chain so that you can reattach the link. You'll need something to serve as a punch pin to use to force out the chain pin. The end of a key ring can be used as a punch pin; if you're desperate enough, use a spare spoke or one from your bike. You'll have to bend the threaded end of the spoke so you will have a short end that will serve as the punch pin. If you don't have pliers, clasp the threaded end with the brake lever hinge and bend the spoke. Place the link that holds the chain pin you want to force out across two flat rocks with the section containing the pin over the gap between the rocks. Place the end of the key ring or spoke onto the chain pin and pound on it with a rock until you can remove the chain pin; make sure that the chain pin is still attached to one chain plate.

To install the chain, remount the chain and put the ends of the chain together. Place a rock beneath the link you want to join. Use a rock to pound the pin in place.

The zip-tie method. If you've lost your pivot pin but have a zip tie with you, use the zip tie to connect the chainplates. Make sure that the tie button is on the inside of the zip-tie loop; otherwise, the button will get caught as it goes through the rear derailleur cage.

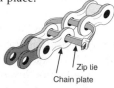

Zip tie
Chain plate

Permanent repair ◆ If the pivot pin is still mounted in the chain plate, remount the chain and use a chain tool to install the chain (see Installing a Chain, in the Real Repairs chapter).

If the chain plate, pivot, or pin at the broken link is missing or irrevocably damaged, remove one or more links so that you can have a sound link to use to reconnect the chain. A bent chain plate may not hold the pin properly and you could easily end up with another broken chain link.

To remove damaged links, place the chain tool on the link you want to break (place the chain on the thin teeth of the tool—the teeth farthest from the tool's drive pin). Turn the handle clockwise until the rivet is flush with the end of the tool. If you have a Hyperglide chain (and you have the special pin needed for reattaching a Hyperglide chain), press the pin all the way out. Now press out the pin where the damaged links end. Make sure that the ends of the chain are compatible (one end should have only a bushing and the other should have chain plates at the pivot pin). Remount and install the chain.

SQUEAKY CHAIN

Diagnosis ◆ Chain or drive train squeaks when you pedal.

Emergency repair ◆ Lubricate the chain with a noncorrosive lubricant. If you don't have any with you, find a substitute that will eliminate the squeak but won't damage or gum up the chain or freewheel. Here are a few choices (the materials at the top of the list are best, those at the bottom are least desirable).

Automotive oil. If you notice the squeak within the vicinity of your car or you are near a gas station, use engine oil. The dipstick makes a handy applicator.

Hand lotion or suntan lotion. Some people claim that the waterproof kind is superior if you're riding in wet conditions.

Water. If a squeak is driving you insane and you don't have anything else, douse your chain with your water bottle. Water is a mild lubricant.

Permanent repair ◆ Lubricate the chain with a bicycle chain lubricant. If you lubricate your chain on the trail, try to clean the chain first. Don't over-lubricate the chain; too much lubricant attracts dirt. You only need to lubricate the moving parts—the pivot pins.

CHAIN SKIPS

Diagnosis and repair ◆ A skipping chain is caused by one of five things.

The chain has one or more tight links. A tight link skips at regular intervals. To check for a tight link, turn the pedals backward (the rear derailleur should first be shifted to a gear) and watch the chain as it runs through the rear derailleur pulleys and freewheel. If the chain kinks at a link, you've found the tight link. To free the tight links, see the next section, Chain Has a Tight Link.

The chain is worn out. It is hard to tell if a chain is overly worn unless you remove it and measure the amount of play in the links, but you probably don't want to do that out on the trail. If the chain has numerous stiff links, bends laterally like a wet noodle, or has heavily worn bushings (the part that engages the cogs), you probably have a worn chain. Replace the chain.

The freewheel cogs are worn out. Look for scalloped edges or hooks in the freewheel teeth. Worn cogs are most common on the gears you use most often. Replace the freewheel. While you're at it, replace the chain. In the meantime, try not to use the gears that skip.

The rear derailleur is bent. Straighten the bent derailleur. See the section Bent Rear Derailleur Cage and Derailleur Hanger.

The index shifting is out of adjustment. Adjust the index shifting; see Adjusting Index Shifting (Rear Derailleur), in the Real Repairs chapter.

CHAIN HAS A TIGHT LINK

Diagnosis ◆ The chain skips at regular intervals. A tight link will cause a chain to skip. To check for a tight link, turn the pedals backward (first shift the rear derailleur to a gear) and watch the chain as it runs through the rear derailleur pulleys and freewheel. If the chain kinks at a link, you've found the tight link.

Emergency repair ◆ Grab the chain on each side of the tight link (put your thumbs on the chain plates) and flex the chain back and forth. To check if the link has been loosened, move the link that was tight at the pivot pin and feel for any binding, or see if the chain still kinks at that pivot pin.

Lubricant sometimes can free a tight link, too. Grit sometimes causes friction and binding in a tight link. Use lubricant on the link at the pivot points to flush the grit out.

Permanent repair ◆ Use a chain tool to unkink the link. If you know how to use a standard-style chain tool, you know that the wide teeth (closest to the tool's drive pin) are used to relieve the binding caused by installing a link too tightly. Place the stiff link on the wide teeth of the chain tool and turn the tool's drive pin a bit (no more than a quarter of a turn). This should free the binding by spreading the chain plates slightly. Don't push the pivot pin out—you only need to relieve the tension between the chain plates.

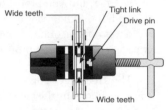

If the chain keeps kinking, replace the chain. Check the freewheel cogs and chainrings for wear, too. If those parts are worn, a new chain by itself won't solve the problem.

JAMMED CHAIN

Diagnosis ◆ The chain is jammed between the crankarm and bottom bracket, between one of the chainrings and the chainstay, between the frame and small cog, or between the large cog and the spokes.

Emergency and permanent repair ◆ Free the jammed chain (see Freeing a Jammed Chain, in the Real Repairs chapter).

Tires and Tubes

FLAT TIRE

Diagnosis ◆ Little or no air in tire. The tube will not hold air.
Emergency repair and permanent repair ◆ If you have a

spare tube or patch kit, fix the flat (see Fixing a Flat Tire, in the Real Repairs chapter).

RIPPED SIDEWALL

Diagnosis • The tube bulges through the sidewall, or the tire has repeated flats due to blowout.

Emergency repair • The key to fixing a ripped sidewall is in finding a strong enough material to reinforce (boot) the rip so that the tube doesn't bulge out and burst. The material should be at least two inches wider than the rip (so that when placed, it's one inch wider on each side of the rip). Obviously, a stronger material lets you use more air pressure in the tire. You want to find a material that is most like the tire casing material—woven and nonelastic. Here are a few good trailside choices (the materials at the top of the list are strongest, those at the bottom are less reliable):

- Duct tape
- Plastic wrapping from a granola bar or energy bar
- Layers of paper. Some people say dollar bills work best because they contain fabric. You could also use the pages or cover of this book.
- A sock or other woven cloth. Cordura or other strong nylon fabrics (from your seat bag or pack, for example) work best.
- Leather. Use a glove, or, if you're desperate enough, tear the leather off of your seat—it should work adequately.

Once you've found some adequate booting material, place the booting material inside the tire and center it over the rip (don't put the tube in yet). If you use duct tape, use the sticky side of the tape to hold the boot in place on the casing. Inflate the tube enough to give it form; the inflated tube will help hold the boot in place while you reinstall the tire bead. Install the tube and seat the tire bead. Before you inflate the tire completely, make sure that the boot hasn't moved, exposing the tube. As you inflate the tire, watch the booted area to make sure that the boot doesn't bulge. Inflate the tire to the highest pressure you can get without the booted area bulging. If possible, avoid putting your full weight on the tire—the lower pressure will make you more vulnerable to pinch flats. Take corners slowly to reduce side-load on the booted area.

If the rip is too big to reinforce (you can't keep the tube from bulging), you'll need to use one of the last-ditch repairs in the section No Tubes or Patches.

Permanent repair ✦ Replace the tire.

NO TUBES OR PATCHES

Diagnosis ✦ No good tubes or patches left (or you had none to begin with).

Emergency repair

If you have a pump and the leak is slow. Inflate the tire to the highest pressure you can. Ride the bike. Pump up the tire again just before the tire appears distorted (flattened against the ground) or before the tire loses its ability to cushion against hard objects (you feel objects such as rocks compressing the tire against the rim).

If you have a pump but you don't have tire levers. Work the tire off with your fingers or with a quick release lever. (See the section No Tire Levers.) Remove the tube from the tire. Find the leak in the tube. Inflate the tube so that it is about the same size as the tire it came out of. You'll be able to hear air hissing out of large holes or tears. If you can't hear the leak, see the section Finding Punctures in a Tube. If the leak is not near the valve stem, cut the tube in half at the leak and tie a knot at both ends. Slowly inflate the tube to give it form. Install the tube and inflate it.

If you don't have a pump. Remove the tube from the

tire. Cut the tube. Tie a knot at one end. Fill the tube full of mud, sand, dirt, leaves, grass, clothing, or anything else rela-

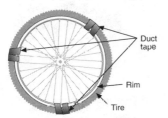

Duct tape

Rim

Tire

tively soft you can stuff into the tube. Pack enough material into the tube to give the tire enough shape to ride. Tie the other end of the tube to close it. Install the tube in the tire, and the tire onto the rim. Wrap duct tape around the tire and rim in three places. Taping the tire and rim to-gether will help keep the tire on the rim. Make sure that there is enough clearance for the brake pads. Start riding slowly. There is no air pressure holding the bead of the tire onto the rim; therefore, it would be easy to roll the tire off of the rim when going around a corner.

Permanent repair ◆ Replace the tube (see Fixing a Flat Tire, in the Real Repairs chapter).

BROKEN BEAD ON TIRE

Diagnosis ◆ The bead of the tire is severed or has torn away from the tire.

Emergency repair ◆ If the bead has torn away from the tire, you may be able to boot the tire. However, the rip may con-tinue to get larger when you add air pressure to the tire. See the section Ripped Sidewall. If the bead is severed, the tire usually cannot hold itself to the rim. Try the emergency re-pairs in the No Tubes or Patches section. Note that if you try the cutting-and-tying-the-tube method, you'll need to cut the tube where the bead is broken. This relieves pressure in the area where the bead is broken and may help prevent the tire from blowing out in that area.

Permanent repair ◆ Replace the tire.

NO TIRE LEVERS

Diagnosis ◆ Broken or missing tire levers.

Emergency repair ◆ If you have a strong quick release lever (steel or thick aluminum) on your seat post or wheels, you can use the lever of the quick release as a tire lever.

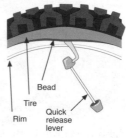

Bead

Tire

Rim   Quick
        release
        lever

However, most tires are loose enough so that you should be able to use your hands to work the bead off. To do the hands-only technique, deflate tube. Starting opposite the valve stem, push the tire over the side of the rim with your thumbs so that you unseat the bead and loosen the fit of the tire. Do this for a two-foot section of the tire. At the spot opposite the valve stem, push the tire sidewall with your thumbs so that you've

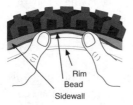

Rim
Bead
Sidewall

pushed both beads to the opposite side of the rim. Push up on the tire so that beads rise over the rim. Push the tire off the rim. Work the rest of the tire off the rim.

If you are truly a barbarian, you can use a screwdriver in place of a tire lever—but you usually put at least one more hole in the tube by using a screwdriver.

Permanent repair ◆ Buy new levers or remember to bring them next time.

TIRE BEAD BLOWS OUT FROM RIM

Diagnosis and repair ◆ The tire bead blows out from the rim, causing the tube to burst or bulge from the opening between the bead and rim. A tire bead blowout can be caused by three things. Here are their causes and solutions:

Improperly seated bead. This is an easy fix; just remount the tire, making sure the bead is securely seated beneath the hooked edge of the rim.

A flat spot in the rim. To repair this, see the section Dented Rim.

A broken tire bead. To repair this, see the section Broken Bead on Tire.

PUMP DOESN'T WORK

Diagnosis ◆ Pump doesn't pump air into the tube. There are plenty of people who've hoofed their bikes out of the woods because their pumps didn't work. The smartest thing to do is to check to see if your pump works before you start your ride—but most people don't check their pump until they need it.

Emergency repair ◆ If your pump is mounted to your bike, this means that your pump is exposed to the same elements as your bike. Before using your pump, clean out the muck, dirt, sand, or other biowaste from the pump head, the pump handle, and, if necessary, the pump body. If the pump still doesn't work after cleaning it, put your finger over the end of the pump head valve opening (where the air comes out) and pump the pump. If you can't feel any air come out of the pump head valve opening, the pump head probably is still clogged. Remove the pump head (unscrew the knurled cap of the pump head) and the pump handle and plunger (unscrew the knurled cap at the end of the pump body opposite the pump head and then pull out the pump handle, plunger rod, and plunger) and clean the debris out of the pump head and body.

The leather or rubber plunger that forces the air out of the pump may be dried out or damaged. Lubricate it by putting a little oil or grease on the plunger. Don't lubricate too much—excess oil or grease can gum up the pump so that the air won't flow.

Permanent repair ◆ Clean and lubricate the pump, or replace the pump.

Wheels and Hubs

DENTED RIM

Diagnosis ◆ A dent in the rim may cause the rim to rub against the brake pads, or it may cause the tire tube to blow out. The dent may be a flat spot or bend in the rim. Flat spots usually are caused by hitting or landing on a hard object with the wheel.

Emergency repair ◆ If the dent does not cause your tire to blowout, leave the rim as it is and try to ride home. Ride carefully if the dent is severe—making turns puts side-load on the tire, and because a dented rim cannot hold a tire as securely as a straight rim, a hard, fast turn may cause a blowout. If you have a severe flat spot, make sure that the brake pads do not contact the tire. If the brake pads rub against the tire, they will eventually wear a hole in the tire's sidewall, causing a blowout.

If the dent causes the rim to rub against the brakes, you can loosen the brakes for that wheel so that the rim clears the brake pads. Most brakes have a barrel adjuster on the brake lever. Loosen the locknut and screw in the barrel adjuster until the rim can pass between the brake pads; you may need to pull the brake lever a few times to let out the slack in the cable.

For dents in the sidewall of the rim, you can use an adjustable wrench to bend the sidewall straight. Most rims are aluminum, which bends fairly easily but is also prone to fatigue; if you keep bending the sidewall back and forth, the aluminum may crack or break. Try to bend the sidewall of the rim as little as possible.

For vertical dents or severe flat spots, you usually can't do much because the material of the rim is actually impacted and compressed and probably can't be bent straight. If the dent is medium-sized (spans two to six spoke holes in the rim) and is a gradual bend (the rim is not crimped, creased, or cracked), you can try pounding the rim back into shape. Note that you risk causing greater damage to the rim by using this technique; you should do this only if the tire will not hold on to the rim (the tube blows out immediately after you inflate the tire). Also, don't try this if the dent is on the seam of the rim; the pounding can cause the rim to break.

To pound a vertical dent straight, first deflate the tire. Remove the nipples from the spokes that are in the middle of the dented area. Move the spokes so that you will have room to pound. Find a log (about 3 to 4 inches in diameter) or board (a 2-by-4 is a good size). Place the log or board in the middle of the dent. Use a big rock to pound the log or board until the rim is straight. Reattach the nipples and spokes. Tighten the spokes. Inflate the tire. True the wheel.

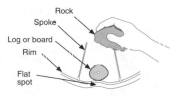

Permanent repair

Small dent: True the wheel by adjusting spoke tension (see Truing a Wheel, in the Real Repairs chapter).

Large dent: Replace the rim.

BENT RIM: BENDS, TACOS, AND POTATO CHIPS

Diagnosis • A small bend can cause the rim to rub on the brake pads. A big bend (rim is twisted into the shape of a taco or potato chip) makes the wheel impossible to turn; it may jam against the frame and brakes.

Emergency repair

Small bend: If the bend is very small and you're lazy, you can loosen the brakes so that the brake pads have more clearance. Most brakes have a barrel adjuster on the brake lever. Loosen the locknut and screw in the barrel adjuster until the rim can pass between the brake pads; you may need to pull the brake lever a few times to let out the slack in the cable. If the bend is large but not a taco or potato chip, you can straighten the rim by adjusting the spoke tension.

Potato-chipped or tacoed rim: What's the difference between a potato chip and a taco? A taco is a uniformly bent rim—folded in half with no twists in the bend, similar to a

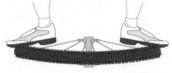

fried taco shell. You can force a taco straight to some degree by applying constant pressure to the folded edge of the taco. You can push against the edge with your hands but it is easier to just stand on the folded edge. Light jumping may help.

A potato chip is a rim that is bent and twisted; it looks something like an infinity symbol. The taco solution usually won't work on a potato chip—it probably will only move the twist in the rim. You may be able to force a potato chip somewhat straight by applying a severe impact shock to the rim. Take out your quick release skewer to avoid damage to the quick release. Find a hard surface. Lift the wheel over your head and throw the wheel (so that it is flat on its side—not on the tire) on the ground as hard as you can. Note: This may have therapeutic value—it always makes me feel better when I've just trashed an expensive rim.

If these potato-chipped or tacoed rim repair techniques get the rim straight enough, you can straighten the rim further by adjusting the spoke tension so that the rim fits between the brake pads (see Truing a Wheel, in the Real Repairs chapter).

Permanent repair

Small bend: True the wheel by adjusting spoke tension (see Checking Spoke Tension, in the Real Repairs chapter).

Tacoed or potato-chipped rim: Replace the rim.

BROKEN FREEWHEEL

Diagnosis ◆ When you pedal, the freewheel doesn't engage— the freewheel only spins on the wheel. More than likely, the freewheel has a broken pawl.

Emergency repair ◆ If you have some zip ties, you can use them to tie the freewheel to the spokes. Alternatively, you can use a toe strap, the nylon cord from a wind breaker, or a shoe-lace. If you're really desperate, you can take off two or three spokes and use them to tie the freewheel to the other spokes.

Note: After you've tied the freewheel to the spokes, you won't be able to coast or stop pedaling. Control your speed on descents.

Permanent repair ◆ Replace the freewheel (see Removing and Replacing a Freewheel, in the Real Repairs chapter).

LOCKED FREEWHEEL

Diagnosis ◆ You cannot stop the crankarms from turning (that is, coast) because the freewheel cannot spin. The pawl has broken and jammed inside the freewheel.

Emergency repair • Leave it alone. You're lucky you can pedal. If you try to break the freewheel loose, you may break the freewheel so that it won't engage and then you'll have to do the "Broken Freewheel" fix found earlier in this section.

Permanent repair • Replace the freewheel (see Removing and Replacing a Freewheel, in the Real Repairs chapter).

BENT OR BROKEN AXLE

Diagnosis • The hub has play. To check for a bent axle, re-move the wheel from the bike and remove the quick release from the axle. Turn the axle. Make sure that the hub is not loose (see the section Loose Hub). If the end of the axle does not turn in a perfect circle (it moves up and down or side to side), the axle probably is bent.

If the axle is broken, the axle can be removed from the hub when you remove the quick release skewer. Don't remove the axle because the two broken halves of the axle will fall out—along with the bearings.

Emergency repair • Leave it alone. The quick release will hold the axle together. If you try removing the axle, you may lose the bearings or get dirt inside the hub bearings.

Permanent repair • Replace the axle (see Replacing an Axle, in the Real Repairs chapter).

LOOSE HUB

Diagnosis • The hub has play. To check for a loose hub, grab the rim (do this with the wheel installed on the bike) and try moving the rim side to side. If you can feel any movement when you move the rim to each side, the hub is loose. A loose hub can cause the brakes to rub on the rim. A loose rear hub can cause poor shifting on the rear derailleur. A loose front hub can cause unstable handling.

A loose hub also can be the sign of a broken or bent axle;

if you leave a hub loose, its axle eventually will break or bend. Check to see if the axle is broken.

Emergency repair ✦ If you don't have a set of cone wrenches, check if the locknut for the cone is loose. If the locknut is loose, tighten the cone by hand until there is no play in the hub. Proper adjustment has no lateral play in the hub axle and no resistance when spinning the wheel. You may want to tighten the cone tighter than the proper adjustment since it probably will work loose again. Tighten the locknut as tight as you can by hand. Make sure that the wheel spins.

If your locknut isn't loose and you don't have any cone wrenches, there's nothing you can do. You can continue to ride the hub.

Permanent repair ✦ Adjust the hub (see Adjusting a Hub, in the Real Repairs chapter).

LOOSE SPOKE

Diagnosis ✦ Loose spokes can be a symptom of a bent, dented, or cracked rim. Check the rim in the area where the spokes are loose. If the rim is bent or dented, see the sections, Dented Rim or Bent Rim: Bends, Tacos, and Potato Chips.

Emergency repair and permanent repair ✦ Tighten the spoke and true the wheel (see Truing a Wheel, in the Real Repairs chapter).

BROKEN SPOKE

Diagnosis ✦ One or more spokes are broken. A broken spoke can be a sign of rim damage, so check the rim for dents, bends, or cracks.

If you have only one broken spoke and you are on a single-day ride, follow the Emergency Repair steps, continue on your ride, and replace the spoke at home; it's not worth the extra time to replace it on the trail. If more spokes start to break, head for home or replace the spokes. If you are on a long tour, replace the broken spokes to reduce the chance of permanent damage to the rim.

Emergency repair ♦ Remove the broken spoke or twist it around an adjacent spoke. If you twist it, twist it tightly so that it won't rattle or shake loose. To compensate for the broken spoke (it may be causing the rim to rub against the brake pads), loosen the two spokes adjacent to the broken spoke by half a turn. You may need to adjust more spokes in that area. For tips on adjusting spokes, see Truing a Wheel, in the Real Repairs chapter. If the brake pads still rub against the rim, loosen the brakes so that the brake pads have more clearance. Most brakes have a barrel adjuster on the brake lever. Loosen the locknut and screw in the barrel adjuster until the rim can pass between the brake pads; you may need to pull the brake lever a few times to let out the slack in the cable.

Permanent repair ♦ Replace the spoke (see Replacing a Spoke, in the Real Repairs chapter).

BROKEN QUICK RELEASE

Diagnosis ♦ The quick release lever or quick release mechanism is broken. You can't open or close the quick release.

Emergency repair ♦ If you have a broken quick release, the safest thing to do is walk the bike. If the quick release fails, you could end up crashing hard. However, if you're willing to take the risk to save some time (for example, impending darkness), there are some things you can do. If the quick release lever is broken or won't open, leave it in the tightened position. The quick release may be frozen in place. If you don't need to take off the wheel, leave it alone. If you want to risk a crash, you can continue riding. If you want to play it safe, walk your bike.

If you're trying to repair a flat and the quick release won't

open, you can do it without removing the wheel. If the flat
can be fixed with a patch, take one bead of the tire off of the
rim, pull out the tube to patch it, and then reinstall the tube
and tire.

If you can't secure or close the quick release, hold the
knob opposite the quick release lever with one hand and, with
the other hand, turn the quick release lever until the wheel is
secure. Pick up the bike and push down on the tire to make
sure that it won't fall off. Ride slowly.

If you choose to ride with a broken quick release, you risk
taking a nasty crash. This is very dangerous—don't do it unless you have to.

Permanent repair ◆ Replace the quick release.

Miscellaneous

BROKEN HANDLEBAR

Diagnosis ◆ The handlebar is cracked (and probably bent)
or completely broken.

Emergency repair ◆ Usually the handlebar breaks near the
stem or at the edge of the bulged/reinforced middle section.
Find a stick that matches the diameter of the inside of the
handlebar as closely as possible. Jam the stick inside the part
of the handlebar still attached to the bike, leaving a few inches
sticking out; jam the other piece of handlebar over the end of
the stick that's sticking out. Wrap the seam with duct tape.

If the break is within the bulged section of the handlebar,
use an allen wrench to loosen the handlebar from the stem
and move the bar so that the break is held inside the stem.
Retighten the stem carefully.

Warning. This repair can be very unreliable—the stick
isn't as sturdy as the original, unbroken metal of the handle-

bar, and the stem cannot hold a broken handlebar as well as it can a handlebar that's in one piece. Avoid putting your weight onto the handlebar. Control your speed on descents; hard braking shifts your weight forward onto the handlebar and could damage your repair and cause a crash.

Permanent repair ◆ Replace the handlebar.

HANDLEBAR AND STEM TURNED IN THE STEERER TUBE

Diagnosis ◆ When the handlebar is turned to go straight, the front wheel is turned off to one side. Stand over the bike to see if the bar forms a 90-degree angle with your front tire. If it doesn't, your steering will be affected—that is, your bars may be turned to go straight but the wheel may be turned slightly because of the bad alignment of the stem.

Emergency repair and permanent repair ◆ Face the front of the handlebar. Hold the front wheel between your legs. Turn the bar so it is straight (forms a 90-degree angle with the front tire). If you can't turn the bar, loosen the stem bolt, adjust the bar, and tighten the stem bolt.

BROKEN SEAT POST

Diagnosis ◆ The seat post is cracked or completely broken.

Emergency repair ◆ If the seat post breaks near the frame, hold the broken piece that is still in the seat tube (so it doesn't fall inside the seat tube), loosen the seat post's quick release lever, and remove that broken piece. You should have enough seat post connected to the seat so that you can reinsert it into the frame—the seat post will just be shorter.

If the seat post breaks near the seat, you may still have enough seat post to reinsert it into the seat tube.

If the seat post has become ovalized so that you can't reinsert it into the seat tube, use a rock to pound it until it is round again. Then try to reinsert the seat post.

If the seat post has a thick wall and isn't flexible, pounding probably will crack the seat post. In this case, find a stick that matches as closely as possible the diameter of the inside of the seat post. Jam the stick inside the part of the seat post still attached to the bike, leaving a few inches sticking out; jam the other piece of the seat post over the end of the stick that's sticking out. Wrap duct tape around the seam.

If you have a seat post that is bent but not broken, count your blessings and DO NOT try to bend it back. Most seat posts are aluminum and probably will crack (and break!) if you try to bend them back into shape.

Permanent repair ✦ Replace the seat post.

BROKEN SEAT

Diagnosis ✦ The seat's clamp, rails, or shell is broken.

Emergency repair ✦ If you have duct tape, you may be able to tape the seat to the seat post.

If the seat clamp is broken, you can use a toe strap from your toe clips to attach the seat to the seat post. Thread the toe strap over the two seat rails and then thread the strap through the hole that was used by the seat post bolt (a leather toe strap probably would be too thick for this). Connect the strap with its buckle and tighten it as much as you can.

If nothing else works, you can wrap clothes around the end of the seat post to form a makeshift seat. If you'd rather not do this, you can simply remove the post and ride home standing up; this is definitely the safer of the two options, as well as a great workout for your thighs.

Permanent repair ✦ Replace the seat.

BROKEN SEAT BINDER BOLT

Diagnosis ✦ The quick release or the bolt on the seat binder is broken.

Emergency repair ◆ If you have a spare nut and bolt, you may be able to fit them into the seat post clamp and use them to tighten the seat post.

Permanent repair ◆ Replace the seat binder bolt.

BROKEN STEM

Diagnosis ◆ The stem body is broken, the stem bolt is broken, or the handlebar mounting bolts are broken.

Emergency repair ◆ If you carried a spare handlebar mounting bolt, now is the time to use it. If you still have one good handlebar bolt and the stem bolt and stem body are not broken, you could probably keep riding—but take it easy on the descents and bumps.

For a broken stem body, you could shim it, but you would end up on your face when you hit the first bump or steep descent. If your stem is cracked, walk home.

Permanent repair ◆ Replace the stem.

REAL REPAIRS

Bottom Bracket

ADJUSTING A BOTTOM BRACKET

Most bikes still use a standard bottom bracket with a notched locknut that secures an adjustable bearing cup. The bottom bracket is adjusted by using the locknut and adjustable bearing cup. Some higher-end bikes may have a sealed bottom bracket with a special locking mechanism such as a snap ring or a special lockring. These are adjusted using a special lockring tool.

Standard Bottom Bracket

Loosen the lockring with a lockring wrench. If you don't have a lockring wrench, use the screwdriver-and-rock technique outlined in Loose Bottom Bracket, in the Troubleshooting chapter.

Tighten the adjustable cup until the bottom bracket is properly adjusted or is slightly loose. Turn the adjustable cup using the small holes in the cup. You can use a pin tool or use the screwdriver-and-rock technique to turn the cup. For proper adjustment, the bottom bracket should be tight enough so that there is no play but loose enough so that the bottom bracket spindle can turn smoothly and freely. After you've gotten the adjustable cup properly adjusted, tighten the lockring. If the bottom bracket is still too loose or tight, loosen the lockring again and readjust the bottom bracket.

Sealed Bottom Bracket

If your bottom bracket has a snap ring that holds the bottom bracket in place, you usually can't do any adjusting.

If your bottom bracket has a special lockring and you have the lockring tool, you can turn the lockring to tighten the bottom bracket. If you don't have the tool, you're out of luck.

Brakes

CENTERING CANTILEVER BRAKES, U-BRAKES, AND POWER CAMS

Most brakes on later-model mountain bikes are cantilever brakes. If your bike is an older model (1980s or earlier), you may have a U-Brake or Power Cam on the rear of the bike. Before you start centering the brakes, make sure that the rim is reasonably true and that the wheel is mounted correctly.

Checking Brake Adjustment

If your rim is straight, it will be perfectly centered between the brake pads. The brake pads shouldn't drag against the rim. The amount of space between each brake pad and its corresponding rim should be uniform and should be no more than ¼ to ⅜ of an inch; ⅛ of an inch is optimum.

In the real world, a rim usually isn't perfectly straight. If your brakes don't drag and you have at least ⅛ of an inch clearance, you should be happy. If you need to have more than ¼ of an inch clearance on each side in order for the rim to clear the brake pads, you may need to true the wheel (see Truing a Wheel). If the clearance is more than ½ of an inch, adjust the cable tension on your brakes (see Adjusting Brake Cable Tension).

Cantilever Brakes

Cantilever brakes have a straddle bridge that holds the straddle cable. If you have an old style straddle bridge, you can move the straddle bridge along the straddle cable to make some minor centering adjust-ments. If a brake pad drags on one side, pull the brake pad away from the rim and push the straddle bridge toward the other side. Squeeze the brakes a couple times. If you overdid it, do the same thing on the other brake pad.

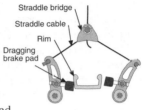

Straddle bridge
Straddle cable
Rim
Dragging brake pad

If you have the new-style Shimano cantilever straddle bridges, loosen the straddle button with an allen wrench, cen-ter the brake by moving the button, and retighten the button.

Shimano cantilevers come with a small allen key (2.5 mil-limeters) for use in centering the cantilevers. The allen key con-trols the load on the spring in the one cantilever. If the cantilever that takes the allen key drags on the rim, tighten the key slightly. If the other cantilever drags on the rim, loosen the key slightly. Never turn the key more than half of a turn at a time. After adjusting the cantilevers, squeeze the brakes. Check the brake pad adjustment. Turn the key again if necessary.

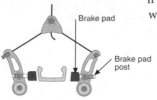

Brake pad
Brake pad post

If neither of the other techniques work, move the brake pad. The brake pad is mounted on a metal post. You will need to slide the post on the brake mount so that it is closer to or farther from the rim. To do this, select the brake pad to move. Loosen the brake pad mounting bolt. Move the post so that the brake pad clears the rim. Make sure that the brake pad is adjusted correctly (see Adjusting Brake Pads). Tighten the brake pad mounting bolt. Check the brake adjustment.

U-Brakes

Shimano U-Brakes come with a small allen key (2.5 millimeters) for use in centering the brake arms. The allen key controls the load on the spring in one of the brake arms. If the brake arm that takes the allen key drags on the rim, tighten the key slightly. If the other brake arm drags on the rim, loosen the key slightly. Never turn the key more than half of a turn at a time. After adjusting the brake arms, squeeze the brakes. Check the brake pad adjustment. Turn the allen key again if necessary.

Power Cams

To adjust a Power Cam, you need an adjustable wrench and an allen key. Usually you adjust one arm of the Power Cam so that the spring tensions of both arms are balanced and the brake pads are centered. If you have a rear brake that is mounted on the chainstay, flip the bike upside down to work on it. Select the arm that drags. Remember or mark the orientation of the wrench flats. Hold the wrench flats with the adjustable wrench. Loosen the allen key attachment bolt just enough so that you feel tension on the wrench. Turn the wrench about an eighth of a turn to increase the tension on the spring. Hold the wrench in position. Tighten the allen key. Check the brake pad adjustment. Adjust again if necessary.

ADJUSTING BRAKE PADS

If you have a small adjustable wrench and a 10-millimeter wrench (most brake pad attachment nuts are 10 millimeters in size), you can adjust the brake pads. You may need to adjust only one, but you should check the adjustment of each one.

Checking Brake Pad Adjustment

What is the optimum adjustment for a brake pad? There are three types of adjustments that need to be made: angle, vertical position, and toeing. For angle, the brake pad should contact the rim surface so that the pad's face is flat against the rim. If the pad face is not flat, it could cause the pad to dive off of the rim. For vertical position, the height of the pad should contact as much of the rim as possible. However, the pad should never contact the casing of the tire. If the pad face is too high, it will rub against the tire casing and cause a blowout. If the pad face is too low, it could cause the pad to dive off of the rim. For toeing, the brake pad should toe in slightly at the front for cantilever brakes. U-Brakes and Power Cams

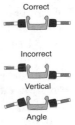

mounted on the chainstays should be toed in at the bottom (the end that points down). This prevents the brakes from squealing.

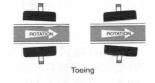

Adjusting a Brake Pad

To adjust a brake pad, loosen the brake pad mounting bolt with an adjustable wrench (but don't remove the mounting bolt). Adjust the vertical position and angle by moving the brake pad. The brake mount usually is mounted in a slotted hole in the brake arm. The brake mount also rotates. Slide and rotate the brake pad mount until the brake pad is flat where it contacts the rim. Tighten the mounting bolt enough to hold this position. Look directly over the brake pad to check the toeing. Most brakes have a cammed lever next to the brake pad post—this is used to adjust the toeing. Make sure that the brake pad is toed properly. If it needs to be aligned more, hold the brake pad mount in position and loosen the mounting bolt again so that you can turn the cam freely. Turn the cam so that the brake pad is toed correctly. Hold the brake pad mount. Tighten the mounting bolt. Check the brake pad adjustment again.

ADJUSTING BRAKE CABLE TENSION

Checking Brake Cable Tension

If your rim is straight, it will be perfectly centered between the brake pads. The amount of space between each brake pad and each rim should be uniform and should be no more than ¼ to ⅜ of an inch: ⅛ of an inch would be optimum. If the clearance is more than ½ of an inch, adjust the cable tension on your brakes.

Adjusting Brake Cable Tension

Use the adjuster on the brake lever to tighten the cable. Loosen the locknut for the adjuster. Unscrew the adjuster one turn at a time and check the brake pad adjustment. Make sure that at least ½ of an inch of the adjuster is still screwed into the lever; otherwise, you risk having the adjuster break or fall out.

If the adjuster doesn't give you enough tension and your brakes are cantilevers or a U-Brake, you can take up slack in the straddle cable. If you have a Power Cam, you can take up the slack in the brake cable. Hold the brake pads together (to do this, a toe strap or a friend work equally well). On a U-Brake or cantilever, loosen the straddle cable attachment bolt (it usually is a 5-millimeter allen key or 10-millimeter bolt). On a Power Cam, loosen the cable attachment bolt and nut on the Power Cam (usually a 5-millimeter allen key and a 10-millimeter bolt head). Pull enough cable through the attachment bolt so that the brake pads are properly adjusted. Tighten the attachment bolt. Release the brake pads.

REPLACING A BRAKE CABLE

If you have a spare brake cable, release the straddle button from the brake arm (on a cantilever or U-Brake) or the cam from the rollers (on a Power Cam brake). Remove the broken cable by loosening the cable's attachment bolt on the straddle bridge (cantilever or U-Brake) or the cam (Power Cam). Remove the cable from the brake lever and cable housing (wind up the broken cable and put it in your pocket or bag). To install the new cable, install the end with the metal barrel on it in the brake lever and thread the cable through the brake lever, barrel adjuster, and the cable housing (make sure you remember to install any ferrules on the cable housing—these are small metal caps on the end of the cable housing). Seat the brake cable housing in the brake lever.

If you are installing a front brake cable, you need to route the cable through a hole in your stem or a cable hanger—depending on which type of cable routing you have. Seat the cable housing in the stem or cable hanger.

If you are installing a rear brake cable, you need to seat the other end of the brake cable housing in the braze-on stop (may be on the top tube or down tube). If you have a cantilever brake and the cable is routed along the top tube, you must either route the cable housing through cable housing braze-ons along the top tube or thread the cable through another piece of cable housing and seat the housing in the cable stop.

Now that you've threaded, routed, and seated the cable and housing, attach the cable to the straddle bridge or cam (the cable goes through a hole in the straddle bridge bolt or cam bolt). Tighten the bolt so that the cable is lightly held in place. Install the straddle cable or cam. Check the brake adjustment. Take up or slacken the cable through the straddle bridge bolt or cam bolt. Tighten the straddle bridge bolt or cam bolt. Make sure that all the cable housings are seated correctly. Make sure that the cable attachment bolt on the straddle bridge or cam is tight. Squeeze the brake lever a few times to stretch the brake cable and to make sure that the brakes work correctly.

Chains

FREEING A JAMMED CHAIN

When a chain is jammed, the simplest solution is to grab the chain and try to pull it out. If that doesn't work, break the chain with a chain tool and pull the chain out. If that doesn't work, try some of the tricks listed below.

There are four places where a chain can jam and each one has its own set of causes. After you've unjammed the chain, be sure to repair the cause of the problem to prevent the chain from jamming again.

Jammed between the crankarm and the bottom bracket. This happens when the chain falls off the small chainring as a result of either poor front derailleur adjustment (see Adjusting a Front Derailleur) or a bent small chainring (see Bent Small Chainring, in the Troubleshooting chapter). Of course, just riding over rough terrain may cause the chain to jam here, especially while shifting or coasting. If you can't pull the chain free, try loosening the bottom bracket's adjustable cup so that the bottom bracket has play. Pull up on the chain while wiggling the crankarm back and forth—the extra play in the bottom bracket may be enough to free the chain. Readjust the bottom bracket after you've freed the chain.

Jammed between the chainring and the chainstay. This happens when there is excess chain slack, when the chain has stiff links (see Chain Has a Tight Link, in the Troubleshooting chapter), or when the chainring is excessively worn. Pull down on the chain and turn the crankarms backward. This should free the chain. If this doesn't work, try the bottom bracket trick used in the previous paragraph. Once you've pulled out the chain, make sure that the small and middle chainrings are not bent (see Bent Small Chainring, in the Troubleshooting chapter).

Jammed between the frame and small cog. This happens when the high gear adjustment for the rear derailleur is out of adjustment. Adjust the rear derailleur (see the section Adjusting a Rear Derailleur, found later in this chapter). If you can't pull the chain free, remove the rear wheel from the bike and the chain will free up.

Jammed between the large cog and the spokes. This happens when the low gear adjustment for the rear derailleur is out of adjustment (see the section Adjusting a Rear Derailleur) or when the derailleur cage is bent (see Bent Rear Derailleur Cage or Derailleur Hanger, in the Troubleshooting chapter). The spokes usually are flexible enough so that you can push against them in order to pull out the chain. If they aren't, try loosening the spokes where the chain is jammed. If that doesn't work, remove the freewheel (or if you have a cassette hub, remove the cassette cogs). See the section Removing and Replacing a Freewheel.

INSTALLING A CHAIN

Before you install a chain, you'll need to know which type you have. A standard chain has rivets that can be easily pressed in or pushed out with a chain tool. A Hyperglide chain requires a special pin to reinstall the chain.

Remounting a Chain

If your chain has broken, it probably has fallen off of your bike. Before you reattach a chain, you need to remount the chain.

Grab the end of the chain that doesn't have a pivot pin. Shift the front derailleur to the small chainring and the rear derailleur to the small cog; this ensures that you have plenty of chain slack to work with as you are installing it. Place the chain on the small chainring. Thread the chain through the front derailleur cage, over the top of the freewheel (mount the chain on the small cog), around the front of the top pulley wheel of the rear derailleur, through the rear derailleur cage, and around the back of the bottom pulley wheel. Join the two ends of the chain together.

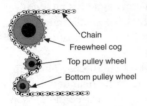

Chain
Freewheel cog
Top pulley wheel
Bottom pulley wheel

Note that some rear derailleurs have tabs that help guide the chain and prevent it from falling off of the pulley wheels. There usually is a tab just beneath the top pulley wheel; make sure that the chain is threaded behind this tab. There also may be a tab just behind the bottom pulley wheel; make sure that the chain is threaded in front of this tab.

Standard Chains

Remount the chain onto the bike. Mount the link in the chain tool. Press the pin into the chain until the end of the pin sticks out the same amount as the pins on the other links. If the link is tight, place the chain on the wide teeth (closest to the tool's drive pin) of the chain tool and turn the tool's drive pin slightly (no more than a quarter of a turn). This should free the binding by spreading the chain plates slightly.

Hyperglide Chains

Remount the chain onto the bike. A Hyperglide chain requires a special pin to join a broken chain. Install the pin tapered end first and press the pin in using a chain tool (you'll hear a click when it is installed). Part of the pin will still be sticking out. Break off the distended end of the pin with pliers. If the link is tight, flex the chain back and forth.

Derailleurs

ADJUSTING A FRONT DERAILLEUR

You usually can adjust a front derailleur using just a Phillips screwdriver. You may need an allen wrench (the size that fits the cable attachment bolt) if the cable does not have enough slack to allow proper adjustment.

There are two adjustments that you need to make: the high gear limit for the large chainring and the low gear limit for the small chainring. If you have index shifting on the front derailleur, you must make some additional adjustments; see Adjusting Index Shifting (Front Derailleur).

The high and low gear limits are set using two screws found on the top of the front derailleur. These screws determine how far the front derailleur pushes the chain when you shift to the big and small chainrings.

Adjusting the high gear setting. Use the screw labeled H usually found outboard on the front derailleur to set the high gear limit.

If the front derailleur can't push the chain up onto the big chainring or if the chain rubs on the outer cage of the derailleur, shift to the smallest cog on the rear derailleur. On the front derailleur, loosen the H screw a quarter of a turn at a time. Shift to the big chainring. Turn the screw again if the chain does not shift or rubs on the outer cage. Make sure that the derailleur doesn't push the chain so far that it falls off the big chainring onto the crankarm or rubs on the inner cage. If turning the screw doesn't seem to have any effect, the cable may have too much slack and you'll need to tighten the front derailleur cable (see later in this section).

If the front derailleur pushes the chain off the big chainring, the front derailleur cage rubs against the crank, or the chain rubs on the inner cage of the derailleur in high gear, shift to the smallest cog on the rear derailleur. On the front derailleur, tighten the H screw a quarter of a turn at a time. Check the shifting. Turn the screw again if necessary.

Adjusting the low gear setting. Use the screw labeled L usually found inboard on the front derailleur to set the low gear limit.

If the front derailleur can't push the chain down to the small chainring or if the chain rubs on the inner cage of the derailleur in low gear, shift to the largest cog on the rear derailleur. On the front derailleur, loosen the L screw a quarter of a turn at a time. Shift to the small chainring and check if the chain rubs on the inner cage. Turn the screw again if necessary. Make sure that the derailleur doesn't push the chain so far that it falls off the small chainring onto the bottom bracket or rubs on the outer cage. If turning the screw doesn't seem to have any effect, the cable may have too much tension and you'll need to adjust the tension on the front derailleur cable (see later in this section).

If the front derailleur pushes the chain off the small chainring or if the chain rubs on the outer cage of the derailleur in low gear, shift to the largest cog on the rear derailleur. On the front derailleur, tighten the L screw a quarter of a turn at a time. Check the shifting. Turn the screw again if necessary.

Adjusting the front derailleur cable tension. Shift the front derailleur to the small chainring. Loosen the cable attachment bolt so that you can adjust the cable tension. Using your fingers or a set of pliers, pull the derailleur cable until it is tight; make sure that you are not moving the derailleur cage when you are pulling on the cable. Hold the cable and tighten the attachment bolt.

Adjusting Index Shifting (Front Derailleur)

The index shifting for the front derailleur can be tuned by adjusting the derailleur cable tension. The key to adjusting index shifting on the front derailleur is making sure that each shift moves the chain to the next chainring and that the chain doesn't rub on the derailleur cage.

Test the cable tension of the front derailleur cable where the cable runs down the down tube.

If the cable is overly loose (has no tension or is hanging down from slack), you need to take up the slack by pulling more cable through the cable attachment bolt. To do this, shift the front derailleur to the small chainring, loosen the cable attachment bolt, pull the cable tight (tight enough to put tension on the cable but loose enough not to move the derailleur), hold the cable, and tighten the attachment bolt.

If you have no tools or if the cable is only slightly loose or slightly tight, you can use the barrel adjuster on the shifter to fine-tune the index shifting. Hold the bike (or have someone else hold it) so that the rear wheel is off the ground, turn the pedals with one hand, and shift the front derailleur to the next chainring.

To make sure that the index shifting moves the chain to each chainring, shift to the middle cog on the rear derailleur and shift to each chainring. The chain should shift smoothly to each chainring and should not rub the front derailleur cage.

If the chain does not move up to the larger chainrings, you need to tighten the cable by unscrewing the barrel adjuster. Unscrew the adjuster one half turn. Shift down to the small chainring and try shifting to the middle chainring. If the chain still doesn't shift smoothly to the middle chainring, unscrew the adjuster until the chain shifts smoothly—avoid unscrewing the adjuster so that it completely unscrews from the shifter body.

Shift up and down between the three chainrings to make sure that the derailleur shifts to each one smoothly. Adjust the barrel adjuster to fine-tune the shifting.

ADJUSTING A REAR DERAILLEUR

You usually can adjust a rear derailleur using just a Phillips head screwdriver. You may need an allen wrench (the size that fits the cable attachment bolt) if the cable does not have enough slack to allow proper adjustment.

There are two adjustments that you need to make: the high gear limit for the small cog and the low gear limit for the large cog. If you have index shifting on the rear derailleur, you must make some additional adjustments; see Adjusting Index Shifting (Rear Derailleur).

The high and low gear limits are set using two screws found on the back or side of the derailleur. These screws determine how far the rear derailleur pushes the chain when you shift to the big and small cogs.

Adjusting the high gear setting. Use the screw labeled H on the rear derailleur to set the high gear limit.

If the rear derailleur can't push the chain down to the small cog or if the chain skips in high gear (the derailleur pulleys align between the smallest and second-smallest cogs), shift to the large chainring on the front derailleur and the smallest cog on the rear derailleur. On the rear derailleur, loosen the H screw a quarter of a turn at a time. The derailleur pulley wheels should be aligned directly beneath the small cog. Shift to the small cog and check if the chain skips. Turn the screw again if necessary. Make sure that the derailleur doesn't push the chain so far that it falls off the small cog and jams between the cog and the frame or makes the chain skip. If turning the screw doesn't seem to have any effect, the cable may have too much tension and you'll need to adjust tension on the rear derailleur cable (see Adjusting the rear derailleur cable tension, later in this section).

If the rear derailleur pushes the chain off the small cog or if the chain skips in high gear (the derailleur pulleys align beyond the small cog), shift to the smallest cog on the rear derailleur. On the rear derailleur, tighten the H screw a quarter of a turn at a time. Check the shifting. Turn the screw again if necessary.

Adjusting the low gear setting. Use the screw labeled L found on the rear derailleur to set the low gear limit.

If the rear derailleur can't push the chain up to the large cog or if the chain skips in low gear (the derailleur pulleys align between the large cog and the next-largest cog), shift to the small chainring on the front derailleur and shift to the largest cog on the rear derailleur. On the rear derailleur, loosen the L screw a quarter of a turn at a time. Push the rear derailleur shifter to push the rear derailleur to the new limit. The derailleur pulley wheels should be aligned directly beneath the large cog. Shift to the large cog and check if the chain skips. Turn the screw again if necessary. Make sure that the derailleur doesn't push the chain so far that the chain falls off the large cog and jams between the large cog and the spokes or makes the chain skip. If turning the screw doesn't seem to have any effect, the cable may have too much slack and you'll need to adjust the tension on the rear derailleur cable (see later in this section).

If the rear derailleur pushes the chain off the large cog or if the chain skips in low gear (the derailleur pulleys align beyond the large cog or the rear derailleur rubs against the spokes), shift to the small chainring on the front derailleur and shift to the largest cog on the rear derailleur. On the rear derailleur, tighten the L screw. Check the shifting. Turn the screw again if necessary.

Adjusting the rear derailleur cable tension. Shift the rear derailleur to the small cog. Loosen the cable attachment bolt so that you can adjust the cable tension. Using your fingers or a set of pliers, pull the derailleur cable until it is tight; make sure that you are not moving the derailleur cage when you are pulling on the cable. Hold the cable and tighten the attachment bolt.

ADJUSTING INDEX SHIFTING (REAR DERAILLEUR)

The index shifting for the rear derailleur can be tuned by adjusting the derailleur cable tension. Shift to the middle chainring. Shift to the small cog on the rear derailleur.

Test the cable tension of the rear derailleur cable where the cable runs down the downtube.

If the cable is overly loose (there is no tension in the cable), take up the slack. To do this, loosen the cable attachment bolt, pull the cable tight (tight enough to put tension on the cable but not so tight that it moves the rear derailleur), hold the cable, and tighten the attachment bolt.

If you have no tools or if the cable is only slightly loose or slightly tight, use the barrel adjuster on the rear derailleur to fine-tune the index shifting. Have someone hold the bike so that the rear wheel is off the ground, turn the pedals with one hand, and shift the rear derailleur to the next cog.

If the chain doesn't move up to the larger cog or skips between the two cogs, tighten the cable by unscrewing the barrel adjuster a half of a turn. Turn the pedals again. If the chain still doesn't engage smoothly with the larger cog (skips or makes a rattling noise), continue to unscrew the adjuster until the chain engages smoothly; however, avoid unscrewing the adjuster so far that it completely unscrews from the derailleur body. If you are running out of threads on the rear derailleur barrel adjuster, most shifters also have a barrel adjuster that you also can unscrew to continue fine-tuning the index shifting.

Now shift back down to the small cog to make sure that you haven't overtightened the cable. If the cable is too tight, you won't be able to shift down to the small cog smoothly.

If the chain doesn't move down smoothly to the small cog, loosen the cable by screwing in the barrel adjuster until the chain engages smoothly with small cog. Shift back up to the next cog. Adjust the tension if necessary. Shift up to the third cog. Adjust the tension if necessary. Shift through the rest of the gears; the indexing should work correctly.

If all the gears shift smoothly except one of the middle cogs, the cog could be worn out. A cog is worn when its teeth have a hooked shape (excessive wear on the leading edge of the teeth). The hooked edge prevents the chain from engaging the cog smoothly and should be replaced.

REPLACING A BROKEN PULLEY WHEEL ON THE REAR DERAILLEUR

If you have a spare set of pulley wheels, you can replace a broken pulley wheel—there is no need to replace both if only one is broken. Shift the rear derailleur to the smallest cog and take the chain off the chainring and place it on the bottom bracket shell; this should provide enough slack so that you can work on the pulley wheels. You may prefer to remove the chain instead. Use the appropriate wrench to remove the attachment bolt for the pulley wheel (some pulley wheel bolts have allen heads, others have standard 8-millimeter bolt heads). Keep in mind how the chain wraps around the pulley wheel so you can reinstall the pulley wheel with the chain routed correctly. Remove the broken pulley wheel. Install the new pulley wheels, making sure that the chain wraps around the pulley wheel correctly. If you put the derailleur cage in its normal position, the chain should come down from the freewheel, wrap in front of the top pulley wheel, wrap in back of the bottom pulley, and go forward to the chainring. Install the pulley wheel attachment bolt and tighten it. Put the chain back on the chainring.

REPLACING A REAR DERAILLEUR

If you have a spare rear derailleur, allen wrenches, and a chain tool, you can replace a bent or destroyed rear derailleur.

To replace a rear derailleur, remove the chain (see Replacing a Broken Pulley Wheel on the Rear Derailleur, above), loosen the rear derailleur cable attachment bolt, and remove the rear derailleur. Install the new rear derailleur. Install the chain. Install the cable on the rear derailleur. Adjust the rear derailleur (see Adjusting a Rear Derailleur, earlier in this section) and the index shifting; see Adjusting Index Shifting (Rear Derailleur), also earlier in this section.

REPLACING A DERAILLEUR CABLE

Remove the broken cable by loosening the cable's attachment bolt on the derailleur. Move the shifter for the cable to the slack position (low gear for the front derailleur, high gear for the rear derailleur). Thread the cable through the shifter, then through the shifter cable housing. Seat the shifter cable housing in the shifter. Seat the other end of the shifter cable housing in the braze-on stop, which usually is located on the top tube or downtube. Thread the cable through the other stops, found on the top tube or under the bottom bracket shell.

If you're installing a cable for the rear derailleur, you will need to thread the cable through another piece of cable housing between the last cable stop and the derailleur. Install the cable at the derailleur's cable attachment bolt (the cable should be placed between the bolt and derailleur body—there may be a small slot where the cable can rest) and hand-tighten the bolt so that the cable is lightly held in place. Pull the cable as tight as you can without moving the derailleur cage; you can use pliers, but be careful not to crush the cable. Make sure that the cable has no slack. Tighten the cable attachment bolt. If you have index shifting, adjust the shifting. Before you start on a ride, do a short test ride to make sure that you can shift into all the gears.

If a cable is brand new, you may want to prestretch the cable before you start riding. Stretch a cable by pulling the cable where it runs down the downtube. Pull only until the cable becomes tight; be careful not to break the braze-on stop. Readjust the cable tension if necessary.

Headsets

ADJUSTING A HEADSET

Most bikes still use a standard headset with a locknut that secures an adjusting race. You adjust the headset using the locknut and adjusting race. Newer bikes may have an Aheadset, which integrates the headset with the stem. An Aheadset is adjusted by using just an allen key in the stem.

Standard Headset

Face the bike from the front and hold the front tire steady between your knees. Loosen the locknut with a headset wrench. Tighten the adjusting race until the headset has the proper adjustment or is slightly loose. For proper adjustment, the headset should be tight enough so that there is no play but loose enough so that the headset can turn smoothly and freely. Hold the adjusting race in place with one headset wrench and tighten the locknut with another headset wrench. If the headset is slightly tight, try holding the locknut in place and turning the adjusting race counterclockwise (this will loosen the adjustment slightly and tighten the adjusting race against the locknut). If the headset is still too loose or tight, loosen the locknut again and readjust the headset.

Aheadset

You use an allen key at the top of the stem to tighten and loosen the adjustment for an Aheadset. However, the stem actually secures the headset by clamping onto the steerer tube. To adjust an Aheadset, loosen the bolts that hold the stem to the steerer tube; these usually are allen bolts. Tighten the allen key at the top of the stem to tighten the adjustment of the headset. Tighten the bolts that hold the stem to the steerer tube. Check the headset adjustment. The headset should be tight enough so that there is no play, but loose enough so that the headset can turn smoothly and freely.

Hubs

ADJUSTING A HUB

Remove the wheel from the bike. Loosen one of the locknuts on the hub (it doesn't matter which one for the front wheel; loosen the locknut *opposite* the freewheel on the rear wheel). The locknut is the nut farthest away from the center on the axle. Loosen the locknut by turning it counterclockwise. Some locknuts require a cone wrench; others are regular nuts that can be turned with an adjustable wrench.

On the side on which you loosened the locknut, use a cone wrench to tighten the cone until the bearings are in proper adjustment. (The bearings are in proper adjustment when there is no lateral play in the hub axle, and there is no binding or resistance when you spin the wheel—see later in this section.) With the cone in proper adjustment, tighten the cone another eighth of a turn. While holding the cone in place with the cone wrench, tighten the locknut against the cone. Check the adjustment again; the adjustment will probably be slightly tight, but this is okay. Now hold the locknut in place and tighten the cone against the locknut. Check the adjustment again. If you have a quick release hub, slight play is acceptable; the pressure from the quick release will compensate for some of the play.

Checking for proper adjustment. To check for adjustment, remove the wheel from the bike, hold the wheel firmly between your legs, grab the ends of the axle with your fingers, and try to wiggle the axle. If you feel excessive movement or a knock, the hub is still loose. Now grab the ends of the axle with your fingers and turn the axle. If you feel the hub binding or you feel bumps or notches as you turn the axle, the hub is too tight.

REPLACING AN AXLE

If the axle is broken, carefully pull the two pieces of the axle from the hub. If the axle is bent, remove the cone and locknut from one side of the axle (on the rear axle, remove the cone opposite the freewheel). Make sure that the bearings stay in place.

If you are replacing the rear axle, look at the position of the cone, spacers, and locknut on the freewheel side. Remember (or mark on the new axle) how far the cone is threaded onto the axle. Remove the cone, spacer, and locknut from the old axle; install them on the new axle, being sure to put them in the right order. Tighten the locknut against the cone. Install the axle on the hub. Install the cone, spacers, and locknut for the other side of the hub. Adjust the hub (see the section Adjusting a Hub).

If you are replacing the front axle, look at the position of the cone, spacers, and locknut on one side. Remember (or mark on the new axle) how far the cone is threaded onto the axle. Remove the cone, spacers, and locknut from both sides of the old axle; install them on the new axle, being sure to put them in the right order. Tighten the locknut against the cone. Install the axle on the hub. Install the cone, spacers, and locknut for the other side of the hub. Adjust the hub (see the section Adjusting a Hub).

Tubes and Tires

Finding the Cause of a Flat Tire

Of all the problems you'll have with your mountain bike, a flat tire will occur most often and is the easiest to pinpoint. However, it may not be as easy to find the cause. If you don't find the cause and take care of it, you might find yourself reliving history. Before you patch or replace a tube, use this checklist to find the source of a flat.

Check the tire tread and casing for sharp objects. If you find something stuck in the tire, it probably is the cause of the flat. Remove the sharp object. If you don't, it will cause another flat. If you can't get it out with your fingers, use pliers to pull it out, or use the corner of a flathead screwdriver or knife to pry it out (try not to cause additional damage to the tread or casing—pry it out, don't cut it out!). If you don't have any of these tools, try pulling the object out with your fingers while squeezing the sidewalls of the tire away from the object where it is embedded. This should bend the tread of the tire enough so that hole in which the object is embedded stretches.

Check the casing for holes, tears, or rips. If you have a hole bigger than one-sixteenth of an inch, use a boot to prevent the tube from blowing out. If there is a tear in the casing near the rim, check the area where your brake pads make contact with your rim. (See the section Ripped Sidewall, in the Troubleshooting chapter.)

If you have U-Brake or power-cam type brakes, worn brake pads can wear through your tire casing. You definitely need to boot the tire. See the Ripped Sidewall section, in the Troubleshooting chapter. You also must adjust the brake pads. See the Brake Pads Rub Against Tire or Slide Off Rim section, in the Troubleshooting chapter.

Check the alignment of the wheel in the frame or fork. Tears or holes in the casing can be caused by the tire rubbing against the frame. When you reinstall the wheel after fixing a flat, make sure that the tire does not rub against the frame.

Check that the tire is seated properly on the rim. Blowouts can be caused by a tire that isn't properly seated on the rim. The bead of the tire must be seated beneath the hooked edge of the rim; otherwise, the tube will blow out from the opening between the rim and tire. Poor tire installation, a broken tire bead, a defective tire, or a flat spot in the rim can cause a tire to not seat properly. When you reinstall the tire and reinflate it, make sure that tire is seated on the rim.

Check the puncture holes. Different types of holes in a tube indicate the different causes of punctures. When you've removed the tube, check it for the following types of punctures:

A small hole: This usually means a puncture from a sharp object. If your other tire isn't flat, make sure that its tread doesn't have the same type of sharp objects stuck in it.

A star-shaped hole: This means a blowout. A blowout can be caused by a bent rim, a tire that fits poorly on the rim, a tear in the tire casing, or an over-inflated tire.

Two small holes (looks like a snakebite): These mean that you have a pinch flat. This usually is caused by low tire pressure, a hard impact, or an impact against a hard object such as a rock. A hard impact may also cause damage to the rim. Check the rim for flat spots, dents, or bends. A severe flat spot on the rim may prevent the tire from seating properly on the rim and can cause a blow out (yet another flat to fix).

FINDING PUNCTURES IN A TUBE

Most punctures are so tiny that they are hard to see. The quickest and easiest way to find a puncture is to use your ears and nose. Inflate the tube so that it's about the same size as the tire it came out of. You'll be able to hear air hissing out of large holes or tears.

If the hole is too large to be covered by a single patch, you should replace the tube or perform one of the emergency repairs in the section No Tubes or Patches, in the Troubleshooting chapter.

If you can't hear the leak, run the tube about an inch under your nose. Your nose is very sensitive to airflow so you should be able to feel the air rushing out of even the smallest puncture. If you can't find the exact location of the puncture, spit on the area where you think the puncture is. The spit should bubble where the puncture is.

Use the piece of chalk that's in your patch kit to mark where the punctures are so you can easily find them when you are patching the tube.

FIXING A FLAT TIRE

1. Remove the wheel from the bicycle (see the section Removing and Installing a Wheel).

2. Place a tire lever between the tire bead and rim and

work the bead off of the rim. If the tire is a loose fit, you can run the single tire lever around the rim to get the bead off the rim. If the tire is a tight fit, you may need to use a second tire lever to pry one section of the bead off at a time.

If you have no tire levers, use the tricks outlined in the No Tire Levers section, in the Troubleshooting chapter.

3.   Remove the tube from the tire. If you have a Presta valve, a locknut may be securing the valve to the rim; un-screw the locknut before you try to remove the tube.

4.   Depending on the cause of the flat, repair or replace the tube and/or the tire. For information on diagnosing flats, see Finding the Cause of a Flat Tire.

5.   Inflate the tube enough to give it form but not enough to be fully inflated. Install the tube in the tire.

6.   Install and seat the bead of the tire. Make sure that the bead of the tire is seated under the bead of the rim.

7.   Inflate the tire.

8.   Install the wheel on the bicycle (see the section Removing and Installing a Wheel).

PATCHING A TUBE

After you've removed the tube from the tire, follow these steps to patch a tube.

1.   Find all punctures. Use the piece of chalk that's in your patch kit to mark where the punctures are. If there are more marks than you have patches, don't waste your patches—replace the tube or perform one of the last-ditch repairs in the section, No Tubes or Patches, in the Troubleshooting chapter.

2.   Deflate the tube. There are two types of valves avail-able, so there are two ways to release air from a tube, depend-ing on which kind of valve is on your tube. Presta valves have a knurled metal cap. Schraeder valves have a recessed pin. If

you have a Presta valve, turn the knurled cap to open the valve, then press down on the cap. If you have a Schraeder valve, press down the recessed pin with your fingernail. You will feel and hear the air escape.

3. Use the sandpaper from the patch kit to clean and rough up the area around the puncture. Make sure that you rough up an area about ¼ of an inch larger than the size of the patch. This roughing of the area helps the glue adhere the patch to

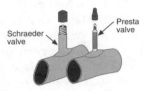

Schraeder valve

Presta valve

the tube. Don't touch the roughed area with your fingers—the oil from your fingers will reduce the adhesion of the glue.

4. Apply a thin coat of glue to the roughed area. Blow on the area to dry the glue; the coat should be thin enough to blow dry in a minute or two. You can inflate the tube to help make the glue dry faster. The glue does not need to be wet to adhere the patch.

5. Remove the foil from the patch. Don't touch the back of the patch (for the same reason noted in step 3).

6. Place the patch on the roughed area. Make sure that the patch is centered over the puncture.

7. Press the patch firmly so that all parts of the patch can adhere to the tube. Make sure that the edges are pressed down (no dog ears).

8. Inflate the tube to test the soundness of the patch. Run the patched area under your nose again. If you don't feel a leak, the patch should be fine. You could take the clear plastic backing off the patch, but it's not necessary.

9. Check the entire tube again for punctures. The new patch will increase the pressure within the tube; this may cause smaller punctures to be more noticeable.

Wheels, Spokes, and Freewheels

REMOVING AND INSTALLING A WHEEL

Removing a wheel. If you are removing a rear wheel, shift the rear derailleur to the smallest cog. If you are removing a wheel that has a quick release, open the quick release lever. If you are removing a solid axle wheel that is secured by nuts, loosen the nuts with a wrench (most front and rear solid axles take 15-millimeter nuts).

If the tire does not clear the brake pads, release the straddle cable for the brake. If you are removing the rear wheel, pull the rear derailleur back to unwrap the chain from the freewheel enough to remove the wheel. Remove the wheel from the bike.

Installing a wheel. Place the wheel in the fork (front) or dropouts (rear). If you are installing the rear wheel, place the part of the chain that comes out of the top of the rear derailleur onto the freewheel (it may make it easier to mount by pulling back the rear derailleur body). Make sure that

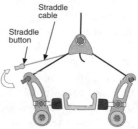

Straddle cable

Straddle button

the tire is centered between the fork or the chainstays. If you're installing a quick release wheel, close the quick release lever. If you're installing a solid axle wheel, tighten the bolts. If necessary, reinstall the straddle cable.

TRUING A WHEEL

Before you start truing a wheel, you need to check to see if the rim is round and straight. You can check the rim by spinning the wheel and closely watching the rim. If it has flat spots, the rim will hop up and down. If it is bent laterally, the rim will move side to side. Make sure that there are no broken spokes.

When the rim is straight, the tension of all the spokes on the wheel should be equal. If your rim is slightly bent, you can correct the bend by adjusting the tension of the spokes in the area of the bend.

Checking Spoke Tension

The spokes should be tight enough so that when you squeeze two spokes together, each spoke moves no more than ¼ of an inch. If you can wiggle a spoke (little or no tension on the spoke) or if you can squeeze more than ½ of an inch, the spoke is loose and needs adjustment.

Tightening and Loosening Spokes

To adjust the tension of a spoke, use a spoke wrench. If you don't have a spoke wrench, you can use a small adjustable wrench. Make sure that the flats of the spoke nipple are engaged in the spoke wrench; otherwise, the wrench may slip and strip the nipple.

To tighten a spoke (with the nipple at the top of the wheel), turn the spoke wrench clockwise. To loosen a spoke, turn the spoke wrench counterclockwise.

If All Spokes Are Loose

If all the spokes are loose but the rim is still straight, you need to tighten all the spokes equally. Start at the spoke next to the valve stem so you can easily keep track of where you started. Tighten each spoke a quarter of a turn. Check the tension of the spokes. If the spokes are still too loose, tighten each spoke another quarter turn. Check the tension. Repeat until the spokes are tight enough.

If the Rim Rubs Against the Brake Pads

If your brake pads drag against your rim at only a few spots, spokes may have loosened or tightened around those spots. Uneven tension on the spokes normally is caused by three things:

◆ Spokes can loosen over time, especially if you ride over rough terrain.
◆ During your first few rides on a new wheel, the spokes on the new wheel may stretch and seat in.
◆ A bend or flat spot in the rim also can cause spokes to be excessively loose or tight (see the sections Dented Rim and Bent Rim: Bends, Tacos, and Potato Chips, in the Trouble-shooting chapter).

If you have a small- to medium-sized flat spot or bend (less than an inch for a lateral bend; less than ¼ of an inch for a vertical dent), you can adjust the tension of the spokes around the flat spot or bend to straighten the rim. You may not be able to get it perfectly straight, but you should be able to straighten it enough to make it rideable.

How do you decide which spokes to loosen or tighten? If you look at the spokes on a wheel, you'll see that half of the spokes attach to the left flange of the hub and half attach to the right flange. When you tighten a spoke on the left flange, the spoke pulls the rim, at the area where the spoke at-

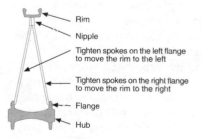

Rim
Nipple
Tighten spokes on the left flange to move the rim to the left
Tighten spokes on the right flange to move the rim to the right
Flange
Hub

taches to the rim, to the left. When you loosen a spoke on the left flange, the spoke lets the rim move to the right.

So, if the rim rubs against the right brake pad, tighten the spokes that attach to the left flange of the hub. If it rubs against the left brake pad, tighten the spokes that attach to the right flange of the hub. Tighten only the spokes around the area of the bend.

If the Rim Has a Flat Spot

If you have a small flat spot, you may be able to make the flat spot round again by loosening the spokes in the area of the flat spot. Loosen the spokes a quarter of a turn at a time. Check to see if the flat spot is gone. Make sure that the spokes are not too loose.

REPLACING A SPOKE

Replacing a spoke is time consuming, especially if the spoke is on the rear wheel. If you've broken a spoke while on a long tour, you may want to perform the emergency repair in the Broken Spoke section (in the Troubleshooting chapter) and replace the spoke after you've finished riding for the day.

Make sure that you have the right length of spoke. You can check the spoke length against another spoke that is on the same side of the wheel as the broken spoke. The end of the new spoke should not go beyond the inside edge of the rim, but the spoke should be long enough to engage in the nipple. You should have no threads showing—but if you have three threads or less showing, this is okay.

Remove the wheel from the bike. If the broken spoke is on the rear wheel *and* on the freewheel side, remove the freewheel (or if you have a cassette hub, remove the cassette cogs). For information about removing a freewheel or cassette cogs, see the section Removing and Replacing a Freewheel.

Remove the broken spoke. If the new spoke and nipple are the same type as the broken spoke, leave the nipple in place. If you're unsure of what type you have, try screwing the new spoke onto the new nipple. If there is no binding and the spoke holds securely, the nipple and new spoke are compatible. If they aren't compatible, remove the tire, tube, and rim strip, remove the old nipple, and install the new one.

On the hub flange, look at the holes adjacent to the one used by the broken spoke. You should see either the heads of the spokes or the bends of the spokes. If you see the heads of the adjacent spokes, slide the new spoke through the hole from the opposite side of the flange. If you see the bends from the adjacent one, slide the new spoke through from the side you're facing.

Now you need to weave the spoke toward the nipple. Look at the fourth spoke from the new spoke and see how it is woven through the adjacent spokes. Use this spoke as the pattern for weaving the new spoke to the nipple. Weave the new spoke to the nipple.

Attach the spoke to the nipple. True the wheel (see the section Truing a Wheel). If you removed the freewheel or cassette cogs, reinstall them.

If no threads are showing on the new spoke and you can't tell if the new spoke is too long, remove the tire, tube, and rim strip and check the end of the nipple. If the spoke protrudes from the nipple, it may cause a flat. Cover the protruding end of the spoke with duct tape or a tire patch. If you have wire cutters, see the steps for shortening a spoke outlined in the following section. If more than ¼ of an inch is protruding from the nipple, the spoke is much too long and you should remove the spoke and true the wheel.

If you removed your tire, tube, and rim strip, reinstall them. Reinstall the wheel.

Shortening a long spoke. If you have wire cutters, you can shorten a spoke that is too long. Note the amount of spoke (number of threads) protruding from the nipple. Remove the nipple from the spoke, and remove both spoke and nipple from the rim. With the spoke and nipple out of the rim, thread the nipple onto the spoke again so that the same number of threads are protruding at the base of the nipple. Then tighten the spoke so that two more threads are showing. Using the wire cutters, cut the spoke flush with the bottom of the nipple. Without removing the nipple from the spoke, clean the threads of the spoke by unscrewing and screwing the nipple on the spoke; repeat two or three times. Reinstall the spoke and nipple on the rim. True the wheel. Inspect the end of the nipple to be sure the spoke is the correct length.

REMOVING AND REPLACING A FREEWHEEL

Before you try to fix a freewheel or freehub, you need to know which type you have (see Tools for Different Trail Conditions, in the Before You Hit the Trail chapter).

If you have a spare freewheel, a freewheel tool, and an adjustable wrench, you can replace a broken freewheel. If you have a broken freehub body (the ratcheting mechanism of the freewheel of a cassette hub), you need a spare freehub body and some special tools (see later in this section).

Start by removing the rear wheel from the bike. Remove the freewheel or the cassette cogs (see later in this section). If you are replacing a freehub body, leave the cassette cogs off, remove the freehub body, and install the new freehub body (see later in this section). Install the new freewheel or cassette cogs. For a freewheel, screw the freewheel onto the hub. For cassette cogs, slide the cogs onto the splined freehub body, screw the cassette lockring onto the freehub body, and tighten the lockring with the lockring tool.

Removing a Freewheel or Cassette Cogs

Before you start, make sure that you have a freewheel tool or a cassette lockring tool and a large adjustable wrench (12 inches or larger). You cannot remove the freewheel or cassette cogs without these tools.

First, remove the wheel from the bike and then remove the quick release from the axle. Engage the freewheel tool on the freewheel, or the cassette lockring tool on the lockring. Reinstall the quick release with the tool in place. Tighten the quick release enough so that the tool stays in place. Use an adjustable wrench to turn the tool counterclockwise. You may need to stand on the end of the wrench to loosen the freewheel. Once the freewheel loosens, unscrew the freewheel from the hub, or the lockring from the freehub body. Remove the quick release, the freewheel tool, and the freewheel (or cassette cogs).

Removing a Freehub Body

Before you start, make sure that you have a 10-millimeter allen wrench. You cannot remove the freehub body without it. Remove the cassette cogs (see earlier in this section). Turn the allen wrench counterclockwise to loosen the freehub. Remove the freehub body.

Index

A

allen wrench: sizes, 20–21
axle: bent or broken, 68, 95

B

bottom bracket: adjusting,
75–76; loose, 29; tight or
seized, 30
brakes, 30–34; broken lever,
34; cable, adjusting, 80–
81; cantilever, 77, 81;
centering, 76; no power,
33; pads, adjusting, 79–80;
pads rub rim, 30–31, 34,
76; pads rub tire, 31; post-
crash, 18; Power Cams, 76,
78; squealing, 32; sticking,
31–32; U-Brake, 76, 78, 81;
worn pads, 31, 33

C

cables: broken, 50; front
derailleur, 87; replacing
brake cable, 81; replacing
derailleur cable, 92–93;
stretched, 44, 46
can't fix, 11
chain, 82–85; broken, 54;
falls off, 38, 39, 51, 86, 89;
Hyperglide, 55, 85;
installing, 83–85; jams, 52,
58, 82, 89; skips, 44, 46,
56, 88, 89; squeaks, 56;
tight link, 57

chainring: bent, 38–40; chain
falls off, 51; loose, 38; lost
bolts, 38
cogs: chain falls off, 53;
worn, 57
crankarms, 34–41; bent, 37;
fallen off, 35; loose, 34;
post-crash, 17; rounded
hole, 36
crashing, 15

D

derailleur, front: adjusting,
47, 85–87
derailleur, rear: adjusting, 88–
90; bent cage or hanger,
48; broken, 49, 50, 91–92;
post-crash, 18

F

fork, 41–42; bent, 41; post-
crash, 16
frame, 41–42; bent or broken,
42; post-crash, 16
freehub, 24, 106
freewheel, 24; broken, 67;
locked, 67; replacing, 106–
107

H

handlebar: broken, 71; not
straight, 72; post-crash, 17;
stiff steering, 43
headset: adjusting, 93–94;

Aheadset, 94; cracked, 44; loose, 43; tight, 43
hub, wheel, 64; adjusting, 94–95; cassette, 24; loose, 68–69

I
inspection, 12–15; post-crash, 15–18

M
maintenance, 12–15

P
parts, 18–28; expedition, 22–28
pedal: bent pedal axle, 37; broken cage, 40; shoe stuck in, 41
potato chip. *See* rims: potato chip
pump, 63

Q
quick release lever: broken, 70

R
rims: bent, 103; dented, 64; flat spot, 104; potato chip, 66; taco, 65–66; worn, 32

S
seat: broken, 73; broken binder bolt, 73–74; broken post, 72

shifter, index: adjusting, 87–88, 90–91; chain rubs, 46; doesn't shift, 44
shifting: can't shift to big chainring, 85; can't shift to small chainring, 86; front derailleur, 29, 34; noisy, 38
spokes: adjusting, 102–104; broken, 69–70; loose, 69; replacing, 104-106
stem: broken, 74

T
taco. *See* rims: taco
tire levers, 62
tires and tubes, 58–64, 96–100; broken bead, 61; flat tire, 58, 96–100; flat tire, fixing, 98–100; no tubes or patches, 60; patching, 100; pinch flat, 98; Presta valve, 99; punctures, finding, 98; ripped sidewall, 59; Schraeder valve, 99; tire bead blows out from the rim, 62
tools, 18–28; expedition, 22–28; for different trail conditions, 27–28

W
wheel, 64–71; post-crash, 16–17; removing and installing, 101; truing, 101–104

About the Author

Tim Toyoshima was born and raised in Washington State. He has worked as a bicycle mechanic, salesperson, and manager in some of Seattle's best bike shops. He started racing BMX in the 1970s and switched to road and track racing in the 1980s. Later he returned to his roots in the dirt and started racing mountain bikes and cyclocross.

Tim also is the author of two computer books, *The Little Excel 4 Book* and *The Macintosh Bible Guide to Excel 4* (Peachpit Press). When he isn't working at Microsoft (or making the bicycle commute between Seattle and Redmond), he is helping his wife, Nanette, chase their son Nicholas, their two geriatric cats, Boris and Natasha, and their dachshund, Franz, around the yard.

THE MOUNTAINEERS, founded in 1906, is a nonprofit outdoor activity and conservation club, whose mission is "to explore, study, preserve, and enjoy the natural beauty of the outdoors. . . . " Based in Seattle, Washington, the club is now the third-largest such organization in the United States, with 15,000 members and four branches throughout Washington State.

The Mountaineers sponsors both classes and year-round outdoor activities in the Pacific Northwest, which include hiking, mountain climbing, ski-touring, snowshoeing, bicycling, camping, kayaking and canoeing, nature study, sailing, and adventure travel. The club's conservation division supports environmental causes through educational activities, sponsoring legislation, and presenting informational programs. All club activities are led by skilled, experienced volunteers, who are dedicated to promoting safe and responsible enjoyment and preservation of the outdoors.

The Mountaineers Books, an active, nonprofit publishing program of the club, produces guidebooks, instructional texts, historical works, natural history guides, and works on environmental conservation. All books produced by The Mountaineers are aimed at fulfilling the club's mission.

If you would like to participate in these organized outdoor activities or the club's programs, consider a membership in The Mountaineers. For information and an application, write or call The Mountaineers, Club Headquarters, 300 Third Avenue West, Seattle, Washington 98119; (206) 284-6310.

Send or call for our catalog of more than 300 outdoor titles:

The Mountaineers Books
1001 SW Klickitat Way, Suite 201
Seattle, WA 98134
1-800-553-4453

BRAKE LEVER

Barrel adjuster
Brake lever
Lever body

U-BRAKE

Straddle bridge
Straddle cable
Brake arm
Brake pad

CANTILEVER BRAKE

Straddle bridge
Brake arm
Brake pad
Brake pad post

FRONT DERAILLEUR

Derailleur attachment bolt
Low gear adjustment
High gear adjustment
Cable attachment bolt
Inner cage
Outer cage

POWER CAM BRAKE

Roller
Roller cam
Brake arm
Wrench flats
Adjustment bolt
Brake pad

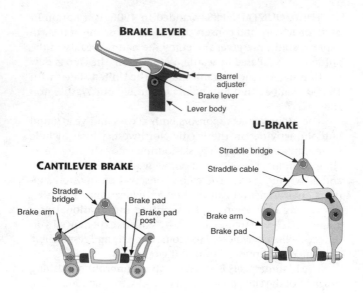

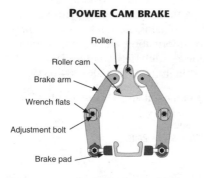

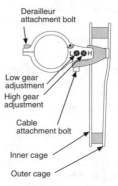